8M

eα

HELGA HOFMANN

# THE NATURAL CAT

## Understanding your cat's needs and instincts

Everything you should know about your cat's behavior

Photographs by Monika Wegler

Voyageur Press

# COPYRIGHT

Translated from German by Wanda Boeke
Edited by Jane McHughen
Printed in Germany
94      95      96      97      98      5      4      3      2      1


**Library of Congress Cataloging-in-Publication Data**
Hofmann, Helga.
     [Katzen richtig verstehen. English]
     The natural cat : understanding your cat's needs and instincts / Helga Hofmann ; photos by Monika Wegler.
                    p.           cm.
     Includes index.
     ISBN 0-89658-255-8
     1. Cats. 2. Cats—Behavior. 3. Cats—Pictorial works. 4. Cats—Behavior—Pictorial works. I. Title.
SF446.5.H6313   1994
636.8—dc20
                                                              94-11132
                                                              CIP

Distributed in Canada by Raincoast Books, 112 East Third Avenue, Vancouver, B.C. V5T 1C8

**Published in North America by Voyageur Press, Inc.**
P.O. Box 338, 123 North Second Street, Stillwater, MN 55082 U.S.A.
612-430-2210, fax 612-430-2211

Please write or call, or stop by, for our free catalog of natural history publications. Our toll-free number to place an order or to obtain a free catalog is 800-888-9653.

Educators, fundraisers, premium and gift buyers, publicists, and marketing managers: Looking for creative products and new sales ideas? Voyageur Press books are available at special discounts when purchased in quantities, and special editions can be created to your specifications. For details contact the marketing department.

Often, while I'm sitting at my writing table, typing a manuscript, a silent black shadow peeks around the corner, fleetingly rubs up against my legs, then lies down in a corner of the study for a little snooze, purring contentedly all the while. My big black tomcat, Mischa, seeks my presence. Sometimes he just wants to be somewhere nearby; sometimes he wants to lie on a warm lap. How different is the dainty, likewise black, female, Jenny. She doesn't much care for human society, comes around only when she's hungry, and otherwise prefers to be by herself. As half-grown kittens, they were both picked up by animal control officials from a band of street cats "gone wild." Before they came to my house, they were anything but lap cats. In fact, they behaved like wild animals: timid, extremely cautious, concerned only with survival. It took months and a lot of patience before, little by little, they placed any trust in humans.

They both helped me answer a question that had preoccupied me for a long time: How natural are our house cats after all this time? At least four thousand years have passed since the onset of the cat's domestication in Egypt. Consequently, thousands of generations of cats lie between the wild ancestors of the domestic cat and our "lounge leopards." To what extent have their inborn behavioral patterns changed in the meantime? Apparently not too much, as my two "wild ones" let me understand. Numerous comparative behavioral studies done by scientists all over the world verify that our house cats still "have a handle" on the whole behavioral repertoire of their forebears. Each sweetly purring lap cat still harbors a predator inside that, if necessary, can make it and survive without being cared for by people. If cats live with people, they do so of their own free will.

This certainly applies without reserve to the common house cat, the animal that has performed its duty as mouser for thousands of years and even today still makes up the greater part of the one hundred million domestic cats worldwide. This nondescript cat is the primary subject of this book. Overbred pedigreed cats are a different case. They tend to be much more dependent on people than their simpler fellows.

There is one thing in particular that fascinates me about cats: their distinct individuality. To describe the nature of cats is just about as difficult, I might say as impossible, as the task of describing human nature—not that of a particular person, but of all people. There is this individual and this other individual, but no prototype. It shouldn't surprise readers, then, that their cat, in some respects, is "completely different" from the ones described in this book.

Helga Hofmann

# CONTENTS

## CAT FASCINATION

### RELIGION AND ART

In ancient Egypt cats were honored as god-animals, and in the Christian Middle Ages they were persecuted as agents of the devil and witches' companions. In popular superstition cats were seen—and still are seen today—as symbols of good as well as evil, according to whim. For centuries the skills of painters and sculptors have been challenged by the beauty and suppleness of the feline body. "Cat fascination" is reflected in all areas of the arts, from Puss 'n Boots to the musical *Cats*.

### ORIGIN AND SPECIES

Over the course of forty million years, the cat family evolved from the first primitive catlike predators to the cat as we know it today: the perfect hunter with a highly specialized set of teeth and a supple body unsurpassed in the animal realm in versatility and agility. Cats were also truly generously endowed by nature with excellent sense organs.

### CATS AND PEOPLE

When cats became pets, they quickly made themselves indispensable as mousers. In days gone by, people also took them into their homes as design accessories and, through deliberate breeding, created various breeds of pedigreed cats. Today the cat is the pet most cherished by young and old.

### BIRTH AND RAISING

Infant kittens are typical "nest squatters" and, at first, are totally dependent on the care of their mother. Most female cats are devoted mothers that can also transform into furies when defending their young. They patiently teach their little ones all they will need to know in later life. At the age of about half a year, young kittens are so independent that they don't need their mothers any longer. The intimate bond between mother and kitten dissolves.

# CAT BEHAVIOR

### PLAYING
### AND LEARNING

In their tireless play, little kittens learn not only to control their bodies, but also gain experience, crucial to their later life, with objects, prey, other cats, and, if they have the opportunity, with people. Cats still enjoy playing even after kittendom is long behind them, whenever their circumstances allow them time to do so. As highly intelligent creatures, cats can learn new things extremely rapidly even as adults, and can thereby adapt to the changing demands of life. In living together with people they are by no means the untrainable loners they are commonly believed to be.
**Pages 70–85**

### THE HUNTER AND
### THE HUNTED

Cats are the consummate hunters. With their keen senses they locate prey; they can sneak up almost unnoticed and pounce in a single skillful bound. Cats play for a long time with their prey before they kill it with a well-aimed bite in the neck. Kittens must be taught how to kill prey or must learn the technique through repetitive catch and play behavior. Most indoor cats will not kill prey, but will simply continue to play with their quarry until the prey is exhausted. Through such play, they vent their pent-up hunting instinct.
**Pages 86–97**

### EATING AND
### DRINKING

Cats are definitely meat-eaters. With their keen-edged molars they cut up their food—whether it is prey they caught themselves or cat food chunks in a bowl—into little pieces, which they then swallow without much chewing. They quench their thirst, as all animals do, with water. To drink, a cat forms its tongue into a little ladle and laps up the liquid.
**Pages 98–105**

# CONTENTS

## CAT BEHAVIOR (Continued)

### CLEANLINESS AND GROOMING

Every day cats devote themselves to grooming their fur extensively, often for hours. The claws, too, are carefully cleaned and regularly sharpened. Indoor cats can easily be trained to use a litter box to do their "business."
**Pages 106–115**

### SLEEPING AND DREAMING

Based on the amount of time spent at it, sleeping is by far a cat's primary occupation. About sixteen and even up to twenty-two hours of its day are spent sleeping. A cat takes great pains when choosing its sleeping places: Above all, the spot must be warm, but it must also be sheltered from drafts and safe from disturbances and enemies. Indoors, a cat sometimes chooses the most remarkable spots for its cat naps. You can tell by its body position if a cat is merely dozing, lightly slumbering, or whether it is pleasantly sojourning in the realm of dreams. Upon waking (but not because of a disturbance), obligatory stretching exercises are in order.
**Pages 116–123**

### LUST AND LOVE

Feline weddings can take place any time of year, although the primary time is in the month of February. Then the nocturnal feline concerts burst forth in unison, and females as well as males often stay out all night to pursue amorous adventures. Should a couple be taken with one another, they gradually draw close during the course of wonderfully complicated courtship rituals, although the mating act itself is quick and seems brutal. However, the decision about whether and when to mate is always up to the female.
**Pages 124–133**

## UNDERSTANDING AND MISUNDERSTANDING

Cat language has a rich and varied vocabulary. Cats communicate with other cats through vocalizations, facial expressions, tail signals, and different body positions. Being the individuals they are, there will be particularly communicative ones among them as well as extremely reticent ones. That we people don't always understand a cat properly certainly isn't the cat's fault. On the contrary, our lounge leopards are usually touchingly concerned about "speaking" very articulately and deliberately to "their" people. They have reserved the meaningful variants of the "meow" especially for us.
**Pages 134–149**

## AT HOME AND ON THE ROAD

Cats can live in various kinds of spaces and in any number of social circumstances. One cat may control a territory of many acres, another is content with a small apartment. One lives as a loner, another as a member of a social feline group, and many develop intimate attachments with people. Some scientists are therefore now talking of the "endless social diversity" of cats.
**Pages 150–163**

## OLD AGE AND ILLNESS

A cat's life isn't all sunshine and frolic. Parasites can become a veritable plague, viral infections can become "cat killers." Kept in an unfitting manner, cats fall ill and often develop serious behavioral disorders. And when cats get on in years, minor complaints often turn into severe physical ailments that can make the final years in people's care ones of illness and decrepitude.
**Pages 164–173**

# CAT FASCINATION

# RELIGION AND ART

The cat is a creature that has always impressed people profoundly. Over the ages, people have deified, persecuted, and spoiled cats. The cat is regarded as a symbol of good as well as evil, entirely according to human needs. Even today, many people still regard the cat with slightly mixed feelings.

What is it about the cat that holds such a fascination for us? Is it the eyes—at once enigmatic and unfathomable, irresistible and touching—in whose deep gaze you can lose yourself? Is it the suppleness of its elegant body that arouses our admiration in the light of day and appears so sinister in its silence in the dark of night? Is it the two natures that inhabit every cat's soul: the affectionate, tender one that the cat exhibits at home; and the independent, mysterious one that appears as soon as it leaves house and humans behind to set off on its nocturnal expeditions? Considering the multiple roles the cat has played in the realm of human imagination from time immemorial, "cat fascination" is not a recent phenomenon. Even our ancient ancestors were enchanted by cats.

## The Cat in Ancient Cultures

Thousands of years ago, in the advanced civilization of ancient Egypt, the cat was worshipped as a god-animal. The goddess Bastet, daughter and wife of the sun god Ra, was depicted as a shapely woman with the head of a cat. The cat itself, her totem animal, was considered sacred. Although it was strictly prohibited for or-dinary people to kill cats, priests killed specially bred temple cats as sacrificial offerings to the goddess. It was not only Bastet, the goddess of happiness and fertility, who was represented as a cat; in the confusing pantheon of the Egyptians, Ra himself, as Osiris, the god of the underworld, also occasionally took on the form of a cat. Because of its mysteriously glowing eyes, the cat was associated with the moon as well. The cat was equal to this heavenly body of the night that shines on lovers.

For a long time, the ancient Germans, who had become acquainted with house cats through the Roman occupation, didn't rightly know what to do with them. They already kept weasels and polecats to combat the nuisance of mice. However, cats, albeit feral cats, had their fixed place in Germanic mythology, pulling the chariot of the goddess Freya, the mother of life and goddess of fertile love. Could a more fitting creature than the affectionate, self-promoting cat have been assigned to her? Freya, who was roughly the equivalent of the Roman goddess of love, Venus, was the most popular goddess of the Germanic world. Temples to her were found everywhere in the land, and lovers asked for her blessing with prayers and sacrificial offerings. One day of the week was consecrated to her and was accordingly named "Freya's Day" or Friday. This was considered to be the most suitable day for weddings, and it took Christian priests a long time to talk people out of their ancient custom of marrying on a Friday. Christ's dying on a Friday hardly boded well for the day, in their opinion. Later, during the prudish and misogynous Middle Ages, which were rife with fanatical religious beliefs, the cat would pay dearly for its association with the ancient fertility deity.

## Christianity and the Cat

Cats and Christianity should have been able to get along. They came to Europe at about the same time from just about the same part of the world, and both got off to a very good start there. The soft-footed ones shared the cells of the first pious hermits and kept the mice far away from their bread.

A typical and often recounted tale from the days of early Christianity, whether fact or fiction, is worth telling here. Around A.D. 600, an itinerant monk came to Rome and stood before Pope Gregory I. To put the monk's humility and obedience to the test, the Pope demanded: "Sacrifice that which is thy most dearly beloved!" So the devout man took his little cat out of the sleeve of his habit.

**Bastet (also Bast or Phastet), the Egyptian goddess of happiness and fertility, was imagined to have the body of a noble, slender cat. Cat images made of wood, stone, or bronze—from miniatures to larger than lifesize—were altar figurines, grave mementos, or symbolic sacrificial offerings.**

Laughing, the Pope waved him aside and likewise drew a cat out of his sleeve. For centuries the cat enjoyed a position of unqualified respect in Christian Europe. The simple people were particularly impressed by the M on the forehead of many tabbies and saw it as the seal of Mother Mary. In the cloisters of several orders of nuns, the cat was the only permitted pet. In devotional works of art, the Virgin Mary was portrayed again and again with a little cat.

In the early Middle Ages the tide turned against the cat. Religious fanaticism, belief in the end of the world, and hatred of the world of the senses and of women directed the thinking of spiritual and secular leaders. In the church's struggle for power, it directed itself primarily against all remaining popular heathen beliefs. It looked for a concept of the enemy and found it in the mysterious, self-willed, indomitable cat. Didn't it suffi-ciently prove its wickedness by flaunting its sexuality with relish? In short order, the church declared it to be a creature of the devil, and henceforth the icy wind of persecution blew its way. By the thousands cats were burned on pyres, either by themselves or together with women accused of witchcraft.

## The Cat In Superstition Over The Centuries

During a time when superstition was rampant all over Europe, largely determining the European world view, the cat was barely able to save its honor. People saw in black cats, in particular, the power of darkness, and people en-countered them with a corresponding sense of fear. (For those who are superstitious today, the saying "A black cat crossing one's path brings bad luck" still holds.)

In a few originally Celtic regions of Europe, cats, particularly those born in the month of May, have a dubious reputation even to this day. They should never be raised to adulthood, it is said, as they become difficult, ill-mannered cats and attract snakes and other misfortune to the house. The origin of this remarkable grassroots belief lies far back in Celtic mythology. May 1 was dedicated to Bile (also Bel or Belinus), the god of life and death, and in general May is held by Celtic peoples to be a month full of bad omens. Is it any wonder, then, that a creature as closely linked with invisible worlds as the cat should arouse superstition and fear, especially if born in May of all months?

In spite of centuries of condemnation of cats by the church, attitudes toward cats have always been full of contradiction. Respect for cats as avid mousers and catchers of rats prevailed, especially in rural areas. This talent also made them popular with sailors. No ship was without a ship's cat; that would bring bad luck! On the high seas, if a ship's cat inadvertently went overboard, it meant the ship was doomed to sink.

Cats were arbitrarily linked with fortune or misfortune in response to people's needs.

**Black cat crossing your path! Even in our supposedly enlightened time, this sight still arouses a feeling of discomfort in superstitious people.**

They were scapegoats for all manner of things, and were offered in sacrifice to appease gods and spirits. Cats have been walled into the foundations of houses and dams (mostly while still alive) to ward off evil spirits and dispel bad luck from the building site. Even up until recently, it was a custom in some regions to send a cat, preferably a black one, in ahead before the residents set foot in the house for the first time. The cat was supposed to draw to itself all the evil spirits that might haunt the place so they would spare the people and the livestock. In some countries, it is said that a black cat brings luck to the one whose path it crosses, but woe to the person on whose path

**Since the Middle Ages, the cat has been associated with witches and witchcraft by both church and lay folk. Countless artistic representations, from later periods as well, verify this. No wonder that the reverse—merely being in the company of a cat—would get many a woman labeled a witch in the eyes of her fellows.**

**LEFT: A color lithograph by Hans Thoma, The Witch (1870). RIGHT: A woodcut by Hermann Vogel, The Witch of the Woods (circa 1890).**

the cat lingers or walks ahead! That signals the worst misfortune. In Normandy, France, a cat climbing a tree, especially a calico cat, was a certain sign of imminent misfortune. On the other hand, a cat sneezing right in front of a bride was taken to be a good omen for the marriage. Although with the conclusion of the Middle Ages this cat craze largely came to an end, many a relic of that era has remained fixed in the minds of superstitious people to the present day.

In European society of the seventeenth and eighteenth centuries, the spirit of the Enlightenment brought with it an extensive rehabilitation of cats. On velvety paws they crept back into people's homes and made themselves comfortable in salons and boudoirs, purring all the while.

## The Literary Cat

Despite periods of fierce persecution, the cat survived over the centuries in European folk tales and legends. And yet, no matter how useful the cat might make itself to people, in most older fairy tales a bad character was ascribed to it. Even in La Fontaine's famous seventeenth-century fables, the cat always embodies evil. However, Charles Perrault, a contemporary of La Fontaine's, helped the cat regain honor and glory with his story *Puss 'n Boots*, a tale that later appeared in Germany in the Grimm brothers' collection of fairy tales. In this story, a cunning tomcat persuades an evil ogre to change himself into a mouse, which it then, as cats are wont to do, devours. With this remarkable deed Puss not only gained both a fortune and a princess as a bride for his master, but also made the race of cats worthy of literature.

At the beginning of the nineteenth century, famous writers such as Victor Hugo, Honoré de Balzac, and Charles Baudelaire began to write down accounts of their cats. The German Romantic author E. T. A. Hoffmann introduced world literature to an epic cat character—Tomcat Murr. Murr, a magnificent feline fellow who has finished his studies and is writing his memoirs, is a prose writer and poet who does not mince words when he describes people and their all-too-human foibles. In this satirical piece, Hoffmann proves himself to be a definite cat connoisseur with great insight into the nature and being of the cat at a time when the zoological field of behaviorism was still entirely unknown.

Poets and prose writers discovered cat fascination by themselves and put it down on paper. Readers responded enthusiastically. This has not changed to the present day. Indeed, contemporary cat lit-

**You bet your Puss 'n Boots! Since he saw the literary light of day in the seventeenth century, Puss has lived on in the hearts of children as a courageous and cunning fairy-tale hero.**

*Cats* is an immensely popular musical. With his rousing music, Andrew Lloyd Webber succeeded in letting London alley cats dance into the hearts of cat lovers all over the world.

The German writer Erich Kastner, known as an author of children's books but also as an author of biting satire and as an astute social critic, was a great cat lover. They were his muses, and he shared his house in Munich with four of them.

Garfield, the "sassy, fat, lazy, and philosophical" tomcat, with his bedroom eyes and insolence, stole the hearts of the younger generation in the United States and abroad.

erature is extensive and varied as never before. A cat rescued from the streets of New York City becomes a beloved companion in the writing of American author Cleveland Amory. Mystery writers place feline characters in starring roles. In general, the character of the cat is acknowledged and its nature is portrayed as realistically as possible. Writers have recognized there is no need to turn cats into fantastical characters in order for a piece to be interesting—they are fascinating enough just the way they are.

## Cats in the Fine Arts

For centuries, artists have depicted cats. Drawn, painted, or sculpted; grim or friendly; alone or in a human lap, they populate galleries all over the world. In traditional Japanese art, they were always a favorite motif. Leonardo da Vinci, Breughel, Dürer, and Goya represented them in their works. At some time in the second half of the eighteenth century, cats became playthings for ladies. We see this change in status documented in the paintings and other artworks of Europe. In countless portraits, the cat becomes a flattering accessory, complementing a dress with a plunging neckline.

With a coquettish expression, the lady fondles the kitty in her lap, toying with its fur. In the following century, the erotic overtones of art became more evident and the ladies' poses more daring. The cat stayed. It had taken its place alongside Venus and Freya again.

# ORIGIN AND SPECIES

The cat family developed over the course of forty million years, evolving from the first primitive catlike predators to the cat as we know it today: the perfect hunter, with keen senses and a supple body, practically unsurpassed in versatility and agility.

From our earliest childhood on, cats are familiar to us. Still, are we really well acquainted with them? What do we actually know about that little creature with the soft paws yet sharp claws who has comfortably installed itself in our homes for centuries? Where does it come from and to what is it related? We admire its perfect body for its elegance and graceful movement, yet how does it function? How keen are a cat's reportedly well-nigh incredible senses? Even though researchers long ago tackled the cat using ingenious scientific methods, a lot of questions are still unanswered, even today. (Isn't it somehow true to the nature of a cat not to surrender all its secrets?) Anyway, what we do know about the cat is astonishing enough.

## The Position of the Cat in the Animal Realm

We are used to classifying animals into groups according to their body shapes. There are worms, butterflies, fish, mice, and many others. The zoologist makes classification even more precise: Each species has a firmly established place in the mosaic of living things. Distant relatives and closer ones are categorized into groups. The hierarchical principle at the root of the entire system always graduates from the simple to the more evolved organisms. Our cat belongs to the most evolved animal group, the class of mammals or Mammalia. The Mammalia, which includes human beings, have hair covering the skin, and the female has milk-producing mammary glands for nourishing the young. Within this class, the cat is included among predators—carnivores or Carnivora, as this order of animals is called scientifically, meaning literally "meat-eaters"—and more precisely still, it belongs to the suborder of terrestrial carnivores. In this group the cat finds itself in the company of martens and bears, dogs, viverrids (civets and mongooses), and hyenas. (Only half the order has been mentioned thus far. The second suborder of predators are the so-called pinnipeds or marine carnivores: the eared seals, walruses, and seals.) Of all the terrestrial predators, cats are undoubtedly the most evolved. Thanks to their physical abilities, the keenness of their senses, and the swiftness of their reactions, as well as their adaptability, they are the perfect hunters.

## The Origin of Cats

On the basis of numerous fossil finds, the ancestral lineage of the present-day cat and all the other terrestrial predators can be traced back to the ancient family Miacidae. They were forest creatures ranging from the size of a weasel to that of a wolf that flourished in the Lower Tertiary period, from sixty to thirty-five million years ago. From North America they spread out over the then Asian-American land bridge, now the Bering Strait, and also over all of Eurasia. In the course of millions of years, the present-day family of predators gradually evolved from them. The miacids themselves, on the other hand, became extinct. The first catlike creatures appeared in the Eocene epoch, a good forty million years ago. Compared with other animal groups, they kept evolving extremely rapidly. Already in the following epoch, the Oligocene, the build of their bodies resembled that of today's cats fairly closely.

One peculiarity in the cat family tree is worth mentioning: the so-called sabertoothed cats. They evolved in different parts of the world, repeatedly and independently of one another. The canines of the upper jaws of these animals were elongated into daggerlike fangs, while the canines of the lower jaws remained tiny or were missing altogether. The most well known of these are certainly the lion-sized sabertoothed cats of the genus Smilodon, which lived in North America during the earliest ice age. They were able to open their jaws extremely widely and, upon catching their prey, they probably used their massive canines as deadly stabbing weapons. They specialized in hunting mammals much larger than they were. For reasons we still can't explain, the sabertoothed cats died out almost completely during the Pleistocene epoch (1.8 to one million years ago)—interestingly, they disappeared from North America and Eurasia at

**There he is, our "yard lion"! Some people also affectionately refer to their house cats as "couch cougars," "lounge leopards," or "patio panthers." The domestic cat's kinship with the big cats is evidently never far from people's minds.**

about the same time. More recent remains have been found only in isolated occurrences. In California, for instance, sabertoothed cats may have been around as recently as thirteen thousand years ago. While the sabertoothed cat sprang onto the scene and vanished again over the course of millions of years, "normal" cats kept evolving. History has proven them successful in the struggle for survival. In the end, they were able not only to survive until today, but they also mastered numerous different habitats.

Of course, cats were never indigenous to two continents: Australia and Antarctica. And they colonized South America for the first time relatively recently, about two million years ago. This has to do with the history of the earth's continental drift. Up until the Mesozoic era, the land masses of the southern hemisphere were joined together and formed a huge continent. About 180 million years ago, long before the cat family had developed, due to movements of the earth's crust, this continent was splitting into several pieces that gradually drifted apart and formed what we now know as Africa, the Indian subcontinent, South America, Australia, and Antarctica. Africa and the Indian subcontinent at some time ended up joining with the Eurasian land mass—and were promptly inhabited by the then-prevalent catlike creatures. Two million years ago, South America, temporarily the last fragment, became linked to North America to create the current double continent, and before long, the cats were well on their way to conquering this section of the earth as well. Only Australia and Antarctica have remained isolated continents to this day. The cat clan had no access to them until the domestic house cat was brought there by ship.

## Our House Cat's Wild Cousins

Although the similarity cats have with the rest of the predators seems to have been clarified somewhat, zoologists' opinions concerning the relations of cats to one another are more divergent than ever. Each new discovery regarding an anatomical detail or the origin of a variety of cat immediately

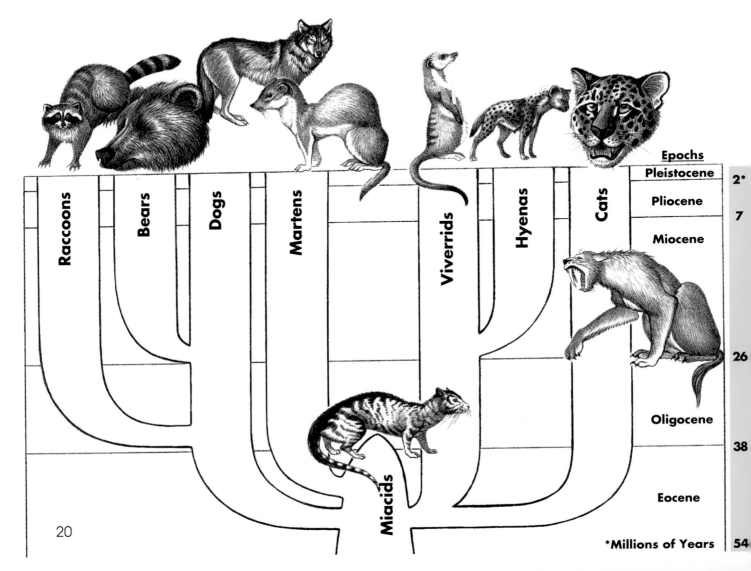

| | Epochs | |
|---|---|---|
| | Pleistocene | 2* |
| | Pliocene | 7 |
| | Miocene | |
| | Oligocene | 26 |
| | | 38 |
| | Eocene | |
| | *Millions of Years | 54 |

Raccoons · Bears · Dogs · Martens · Viverrids · Hyenas · Cats · Miacids

leads to a regrouping, restructuring, and reordering of the felid system. Because there are still so many gaps in our knowledge of feral cats, it seems clear that classifying them will remain a point of contention in mammalian research for a long time to come.

What is known is that there are a few dozen varieties of cats living today in the countries of the Old and New worlds. (Some zoologists count

forty-one varieties, and others group them together into thirty-eight or even thirty-five varieties.) The body structure of all cats is so similar that it is not difficult even for an amateur to recognize them without a doubt as members of the cat family. The most obvious differences between the varieties lie in their physical size, as well as in the coloring or marking of their coats.

**ABOVE LEFT: The lynx (*Felis lynx*) was once to be found across almost all of Europe; now it is threatened with extinction there. Despite its impressive size, it belongs to the family of lesser or small cats.**

**BELOW LEFT: The ocelot (*Leopardus pardalis*) was heavily hunted for its fur because of the vivid markings on its coat, which was long prized in the fashion world. Today its continued existence is endangered in large areas of its native homeland, the forests of Central and South America.**

**ABOVE RIGHT: The cheetah (*Acinonyx jubatus*) is an**

outsider in the cat family. It cannot retract its claws and its body build is otherwise reminiscent of a long-legged dog. With the ability to sprint at speeds of up to seventy-five miles (120 kilometers) per hour, it qualifies as the fastest mammal in the world.

**BELOW RIGHT: The wildcat, or more accurately the European forest wildcat (*Felis sylvestris sylvestris*), closely resembles an "everyday" domestic tabby but is not of the same original form as our house cat.**

**Over the course of millions of years, present-day terrestrial predators, among them the cats, evolved from the family of miacids.**

## Big and Small Cats

Generally, the big cats—such as the lion, tiger, leopard, and jaguar—are distinguished from all other cat species (referred to as "small" or "lesser" cats) on the basis of certain anatomical features and physical postures. One of the distinguishing features is the development of the hyoid bone, a thin span of bone that anchors the base of the tongue and supports the larynx. In big cats, a section of the hyoid bone consists of elastic cartilage instead of bone. This enables big cats to roar loudly. In small cats, however, the hyoid bone is completely osseous. As a result, small cats cannot roar, but instead purr when breathing in and out. Another difference between small cats and big cats is the shape of the pupils. In small cats, the pupils narrow to slits in bright light, as we know from watching house cats. In big cats, the pupils remain round when they contract. Still, there are exceptions and transitional forms to this point of distinction. Physical posture can be equally unreliable as a distinguishing criterion. Typically, a small cat at rest tucks its front paws under its chest and curls its tail gracefully around its body. A big cat lies at rest with its forepaws stretched out in front and its tail extended straight back. Big cats eat lying down, while small cats eat standing in a crouched position.

Cats really do not make it easy for us to bring a plausible order to the classification of their interrelationships. The shy Himalayan snow leopard, for example, is classified as a big cat, even though it can't roar and eats in the crouched posture of the lesser cats. The Southeast Asian clouded leopard can be said to have the characteristics of the big cats, as well as those of the small cats, and constitutes a likely link between the two groups. On the other hand, such imposing cats as the lynx or the puma will have to put up with being classified as small cats according to the previously described criteria.

## The Cheetah as a Special Case

The cheetah holds a truly exceptional position in the cat family. Zoologists have given the cheetah its own subfamily alongside the real cats because the cheetah cannot retract its claws. When it walks, its claws touch the ground as a dog's do, with the result that its claws are dulled. In addition, the cheetah appears to be the only cat that does not occupy and defend an established territory.

# The Cat, the Consummate Mammal

In 1881, the British zoologist St. George Mivart wrote that the cat was "the bloom and the peak of the mammalian family tree." Even though such an assessment might be utterly unfounded from a contemporary scientific point of view, it still reflects the wonder that most people experience when they regard the supple movements and remarkable physical control of the cat.

There is one respect, in which the cat is undoubtedly unsurpassed: its physical versatility. It is a master not only of leaping, climbing, balancing, stalking, and sprinting, but also of acrobatic physical contortion, of making itself small, of lightning-quick reactions as well as of slow-motion movement. Because of the perfect interaction between its highly developed nervous system and its powerful, effective musculature, the cat is the hunter par excellence. Let's look at the body of a cat in greater detail. The familiar "everyday" house cat will serve as an illustration.

## Skeleton and System of Movement

The skeleton provides the framework for the cat's body. It consists of 240 separate bones, and its basic structure is like that of all vertebrates: At one end of the central spinal column is the skull and the other end tapers into a tail (which, in the case of the cat, can consist of up to twenty-six vertebrae). The four limbs join the spinal column at the shoulder and pelvic girdles. Most of the bones are connected to one another by cartilage and joints. This ensures the body's mobility. More than five hundred large and small muscles control body movement. Via neural pathways, the muscles are in contact with the brain. Here all the nerve signals that originate from the various sense organs come together. The highly developed cat brain reacts at lightning speed. It analyzes, compares, reckons, and assesses sensory impressions in order to send com-

mands instantaneously to the muscles so they will contract or extend in a coordinated and useful fashion.

Cats are tip-toers. This means they don't carry their weight on the soles of their feet the way we do, but just on their toes. The heels are clearly visible on the hind legs, like a "knee" bent backward. The actual knee bends at the level of the lower abdominal wall. Cats have five toes on their

**ABOVE: Just like our domestic cats, lions (*Panthera leo*) also prefer to spend the day indulging in their passion: sleep. In the wild, hunger finally chases sleep away and it is time to hunt. In the zoo, however, they can doze to their heart's content and still get plenty to eat.**

**CENTER: Representing a link between small and big cats is the Southeast Asian clouded leopard (*Neofelis nebulosa*). In its physical structure, as well as in its behavior, it combines characteristics of both groups.**

**BELOW: Despite its considerable size, the classification of the snow leopard or ounce (*Uncia uncia*) with the big cats is open to question. For instance, instead of roaring, it purrs like a small cat.**

**The tiger (*Panthera tigris*) without a doubt belongs to the big cats. In its Siberian subspecies, it is indeed the largest of all cats. Its clearly defined stripes are only striking up close; in the bush or tall grass they provide an outstanding camouflage pattern. Sadly, the tiger is gravely endangered.**

forepaws, but their thumbs are so shortened that they no longer touch the ground. The hind paws have only four toes; the fifth hind toe has degenerated completely. Thick pads distribute the body's weight evenly over all the toes. This is why cats can move so silently.

In humans and in most animals, the two clavicles connect the shoulder blades to the sternum. In cats, the clavicles have degenerated to tiny, useless bones. As a result, the forelegs have no firm bone connection to the pectoral girdle but are held in place

**ABOVE: When hunting for such nimble and wary prey as mice or birds, the cat's considerable jumping power is put to good use. Cats can jump five times their own height—from a standstill.**

**CENTER: The skeleton of a cat consists of slightly more than 240 separate bones (and bonelets). The anatomy of its extremities confirms that the cat is a "tip-toer."**

**BELOW: By contracting or releasing an elastic sinew (flick!), the cat can extend its claws in a flash or keep them withdrawn in the pouch of skin between the joints of its front toes.**

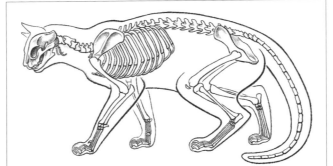

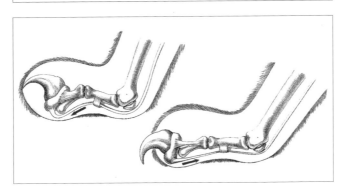

only by strong muscles and tendons. This means the cat is constructed perfectly for jumping lightly down from or springing up onto a surface from a good distance. In addition, this construction permits free movement of the shoulder blades and forelegs, including movement to the sides. This flexibility is an invaluable advantage when climbing, as the cat can simply "embrace" a tree trunk. The narrow thorax and this mobility of the legs also allow the cat to place its paws very close together or even in a straight line, one in front of the other. This is useful for maneuvering in tight spaces or for balancing on branches or beams.

## The Cat's Skin and Fur

Like an oversized sweater, a cat's skin fits quite loosely. The skin moves easily and is extremely elastic. This proves to be an invaluable advantage when cats defend themselves in hand-to-hand combat (or rather, paw-to-tooth combat) with rivals or struggling prey. Because of the looseness and elasticity of their coats, the wounds they sustain are mostly superficial and limited to the skin.

The skin contains a tight network of blood vessels and nerves. Numerous sensory cells register each touch, as well as heat and cold, with extreme sensitivity. Then there are also millions of hairs rooted in the skin. The fur serves an immensely important protective function for the cat. It protects against the cold, skin wounds, sunburn, and too much heat. Tiny muscles located in the skin at the base of each hair can be used to raise the hairs, making the coat appear thicker and increasing its insulating capacity. The cat's body thus appears bigger and more imposing, an effect that an aggressive or frightened cat wishes to achieve when it makes its fur stand on end to intimidate an opponent.

Also to be found in the skin are innumerable sebaceous glands linked to the hair roots. They produce a fatty substance that gets distributed over the fur when the cat licks itself, lending the fur its silky sheen. Skin and hair are both impregnated so effectively that in rainy weather the cat hardly ever gets soaked through to the skin. In addition, the secretion of the sebaceous glands (the sebum) contains small amounts of cholesterol, which is transformed by sunlight into vitamin D. In the daily grooming of its fur, the cat takes up this crucial vitamin with its tongue.

It is often claimed that cats have no sweat glands and that they can't sweat. This isn't entirely true. It is true that the sweat glands in the skin underneath the fur are atrophied, but between the toe pads, on the lips, and at the angle of the jaw there are well-developed sweat glands. The amount of sweat they produce is, however, far too little to provide a noticeable cooling effect to an overheated body. This function is taken over primarily by panting and by saliva distributed over the fur while washing (see the chapter "Cleanliness and Grooming").

A cat's fur is made up of various kinds of hair of distinct lengths. Long straight guard hair and slightly shorter coarse hair together make up the outer or guard coat; fine, fluffy wool hair makes up the thick, soft undercoat. The downy undercoat is particularly efficient in insulating body heat. In comparison with exclusively indoor cats, outdoor cats have much thicker undercoats, which are even denser in the colder seasons than in the summertime.

At the base of the hairs are color-producing cells that constantly manufacture microscopically small grains of pig-

**House cats come in a particularly wide variety of colors and patterns. In many places calico, or tricolored, cats are considered to bring good luck.**

ment. These grains are deposited and stored in the hair shafts as the hair is growing. From this pigment, the entire palette of possible fur coloration and patterns is mixed from two kinds of melanin—black eumelanin and orange-brown phaeomelanin—that are evident in distinct concentrations and blended ratios in the hair. A hair entirely without pigmentation grows out white.

The cat also has extremely specialized hairs known in technical language as vibrissae: long, stiff, yet flexible, tactile hairs. We know them as whiskers. The tactile hairs are extraordinarily sensitive sensory organs that register the least touch. Besides being located on the upper lip, tactile hairs are also found on the cheeks, above the eyes, on the chin, and on the backs of the cat's forelegs.

You might be surprised to find the claws mentioned here in relation to the skin. They are, however, keratinous structures produced by the outer skin in the same way as, for example, a horse's hoof or our own fingernails. A feature typical of cats is the ability to extend their claws in a flash when needed by tensing special muscles, whereas when at rest they are retracted into claw sheaths by a refined sinew mechanism. That is why the claws don't touch the ground when the cat walks and therefore are not dulled. The needle-sharp claws of the front paws, in particular, are not only very effective weapons when it comes to fighting, but important aids when climbing and also when catching and holding prey. The claws of the back paws are also utilized as "spikes" when accelerating and leaping, but they are usually less sharp than the front claws. Cats' claws, like our fingernails, are constantly growing. From time to time they will lose their outer hulls, which peel off. The cat facilitates this by nibbling at them and scratching (see the chapter "Cleanliness and Grooming"). The claw then appearing from under the old one is once again "as good as new," pointed and sharp.

**Thanks to their sharp claws, cats are excellent climbers. From kittenhood on they learn and practice the art of climbing up the trunks of trees. Going back down doesn't look quite as elegant. They can't go down headfirst, so they descend backward step by step.**

## A Predator's Teeth

Show me your teeth and I'll tell you who you are. The teeth of an animal always reflect its diet. Predators like the cat have knifelike canines at their disposal. These teeth are also referred to as fangs, from the German word *Fangzähnen* (literally "catching-teeth"), because cats use them to catch, hold fast, and kill wriggling, struggling prey. The back teeth are pointed, angular, and sharp-edged and are used for cutting up meat. The particular highly developed tools for this are the so-called premolars,

meaning the last upper premolars and the first lower molars (cats have only one on each side of their lower jaw). The crowns of both these "ripping teeth," or carnassials, grip like triangularly sharpened knives fitting tightly inside one another from above and below. The cat uses these teeth like scissors to cut up pieces of meat and crush smaller bones. The cat has six tiny incisors in

each jaw. Other than using them to scrape the remains of flesh from thicker bones, the cat hardly uses these teeth for eating at all. For the care of skin and fur, on the other hand, they are quite serviceable. The skill with which a cat can catch fleas in its fur with them is quite unbelievable.

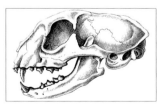

**When you look at a cat's teeth, the long, pointed canines (or fangs) are especially noticeable.**

**LEFT: When climbing on thin branches, a good sense of balance isn't the only thing that counts; a secure grip is also necessary. Claws offer the cat invaluable assistance in gripping, especially when snow and ice make it slippery as well.**

**RIGHT: A cat takes caring for its claws just as seriously as caring for its fur. Through regular nibbling, it removes the dirt sticking to them. From time to time, the worn outermost layers of the keratinous husks are also removed in the process.**

## The Internal Organs

As with the teeth, the digestive organs of the cat are completely geared to the ingestion of meat. The stomach, when full, reaches the size of a woman's fist. (From this can be deduced, as a general rule of thumb, the most a cat can eat at any one time.) The digestive juices produced by the stomach are so strong they even dissolve bones. The cat's intestines, like those of all meat-eaters, are comparatively short. The large intestine is about three to four times the length of the cat's body. (For comparison, the herbivorous cow has a large intestine at least twenty times the length of its body.)

The cat is not particularly suited to aerobics. Compared with its size, its heart is rather small and, as far as pumping power and stamina are concerned, not terribly powerful. To keep pumping about half a gallon (a quarter of a liter) of blood through the body, the heart (at rest) must beat about 110 to 130 times a minute. Air is inhaled into the lungs, and there the blood is charged with oxygen, which it transports to all parts of the body. On its way back to the lungs, the blood takes up carbon dioxide from the body cells, which is then eliminated by the lungs when the cat exhales. A cat at rest breathes about twenty to thirty times a minute. In addition, the blood transports nutrients and waste materials in the body. Most waste substances are filtered out of the blood by the kidneys (two bean-shaped organs in the lumbar region on the ventral aspect of the spine) and deposited in the urine. The kidneys regulate the body's water balance. When needed, they can concentrate the urine somewhat to reduce the elimination of water. The liver, as well as the spleen, located on the ventral aspect of the cat's body in the upper left of the abdominal cavity, are essential for ridding the body of poisons.

## The Cat's Senses

Nature was truly generous when it endowed the cat with its excellent sensory organs.

**The cat's most important sensory organs are located in its head: eyes, ears, nose, and whiskers. Scientists today know pretty well in which portions of the brain not only sensory perceptions but also moods and motor control are located.**

Each of the cat's five senses win top honors in the animal realm. They are so superior, the cat is frequently even ascribed a sixth sense.

## The Eyes

The cat's power of sight is its keenest sense. In total darkness, though, the cat sees as much as we do—namely, nothing at all. In half-light or in moonlight, however, it is head and shoulders above us. Cat eyes can perform in light that is six times weaker than what human eyes can perform in. As with most nocturnally active creatures, behind the cat's retina lies a layer of cells that functions like a kind of mirror, reflecting the incoming light. This enhances the perceptional accuracy of the eye immensely. In extremely dim light, this means that the sensory cells in the retina have a second chance to register light that may have escaped them on the first pass. We can clearly see the effect of this reflecting layer (the tapetum lucidum) behind the retina when a cat's eyes light up at night like two little rays of light, for example, in the headlights of a car.

**ABOVE: The cat's body is not built for the endurance needed for long, mad chases. It is much more specialized for the explosive displays of power needed for quick sprints or huge leaps.**

**CENTER: The cat's teeth leave no room for doubt: We're dealing with a predator here. With knifelike canines (or fangs), it can hold prey fast and quickly kill it. The jagged crowns of the molars and premolars do not grind up food, instead they cut it up. The tiny incisors, on the other hand, serve at most to scrape meat off larger bones when eating.**

**BELOW: Not only the teeth, but also the internal organs and metabolism of a cat are typical of meat-eaters. However, every cat regularly ingests a limited amount of vegetable fare, in the form of the stomach and intestinal contents of its prey.**

**LEFT:** Who can resist the fascination that radiates from cats' eyes? The coloration of the iris runs from copper tones through a variety of yellow tones, from amber hues to green.

**CENTER:** Did you know kittens all have blue eyes for the first weeks of their lives? Starting at the tenth or twelfth week they gradually gain their own eye color, although the true coloration of the iris is not definite until their second year.

**RIGHT:** At night even the dimmest illumination makes the eyes of a cat light up like small rays of light. A reflecting layer behind the retina casts the incoming light back through it, considerably improving visual accuracy.

For some breeds, for example, Siamese cats (large picture), blue eyes are typical.

The pupil regulates the incoming quantity of light like the aperture of a camera. In dim light, it widens to a large, black roundel that almost swallows up the entire iris; in bright sunlight, it contracts to a narrow, vertical slit. The type of sensory cells that react with such great sensitivity in low light unfortunately don't work well in daylight. Thus, a second kind of sensory cell, of which there are relatively few in a cat's eye, has to jump into action. This means cats probably see less clearly than we do during the day. These cells are best at registering movement; they don't perceive things at a standstill very well.

Cats focus on objects most sharply at a distance of six and one-half to twenty feet (two to six meters). The cornea bulges well toward the front, allowing each eye to cover an angle of vision of at least two hundred degrees. The cat doesn't have to move either its eyes or its head to look sideways. Particularly important, however, is the extraordinarily large field to the front that both eyes cover together, since only in this so-

called binocular field of vision is spatial perception possible. And depth perception is a prerequisite for a precise aim—indispensable for a cat pouncing on a mouse.

For a long time people thought cats were completely color blind. This opinion has been proven wrong. Cats can distinguish colors very well, but probably only blue and green, and possibly yellow. Most research has indicated that cats have no appreciation for reddish tones.

## The Ears

The sense of hearing ranks as the second most acute of the cat's senses. It surpasses ours by far.

The cat can perceive the slightest sounds, even ones completely nonexistent to our ears. It hears not only the pitter-patter of mice feet or the faraway squeaking of a mouse, it can also localize the noises precisely and estimate how far away they are. The fine interplay of its ears betrays its attentive listening. More than twenty muscles move each of the two large sound funnels on its head separately and direct them precisely at the origin of the sound. The cat hears not only much fainter tones than we do, but also much higher ones. Mice usually communicate with one another by means of low utterances with a frequency of around forty kilohertz. We don't pick up anything of this mouse talk, as human hearing in the higher frequency range extends at most to around twenty kilohertz. In comparison, cats hear tones up to a frequency of sixty-five kilohertz—and this includes the whispering of mice. This greater sensitivity of the cat's ear to high tones also explains why cats definitely detest shrill sounds with lots of overtones. In the lower tones (down to about twenty to thirty hertz), humans and cats can perceive sounds almost equally well.

The sense of balance, which is located in the inner ear, is also very well developed in cats. It allows a cat to balance instinctively and confidently on fences or beams. A cat rarely falls off anything, but occasionally it happens. Then, it automatically twists its body around as far as its balancing organ tells it to—until up is up and down is down again—and presto, the cat lands solidly on all fours. Some term this feat the "air-righting reaction." (Despite this ability, a cat can seriously injure itself, especially when falling from an unnaturally great height, such as from the balcony of an apartment building. The cat's body wasn't built for high rises and hard asphalt.)

## The Sense of Touch

We introduced the tactile hairs in the section on skin and fur. At the base of each of these vibrissae are numerous nerve endings that instantly register every vibration and each bending of a hair. The cat uses them as efficient feelers when, for instance, it slips through a narrow, dark opening. The long whiskers on the upper lip are extremely important to a cat. With them it investigates objects that are too close to its muzzle for it to focus on. These vibrissae are so sensitive they can register even the minutest currents and vibrations in the

**The ever-changing shape of the pupil gives cats' eyes many different looks. Like the aperture of a camera, the pupil regulates the amount of incoming light. In half-light it widens into a large black roundel (LEFT), to contract by degrees with increasing brightness (CENTER), until in bright sunlight only a narrow vertical slit is left (RIGHT). In extreme situations, the opening of the pupil can be almost completely closed in the middle. Then light enters through two elongated openings above and below into the interior of the eye. The expansion or contraction of the pupil is controlled by tiny muscles in the iris.**

**ABOVE:** The sense of balance is located in the inner ear. It is particularly well developed in cats and facilitates their sure-footed passage over narrow branches or beams.

**CENTER:** Hearing is the cat's second sharpest sense after the power of sight. The cat's perked-up ear funnels act like hearing trumpets that can be precisely maneuvered and aimed at the exact location of a sound source. Each ear can be moved independently.

**BELOW:** The long, stiff tactile hairs on the upper lip are sensitive feelers for close-range work. With their help the cat can, for instance, check the movements of a captive mouse it is carrying in its mouth.

air. The primary function of the long tactile hairs over the eyes is to protect the eyes. In the dark, if the cat is about to bump into a twig, these hairs are encountered first. Immediately, a reflex to close the eyelids is triggered.

## Smelling and Tasting

In comparison with the long nose of the champion sniffer, the dog, the nose of a cat seems pretty tiny. This might make you think the cat's sense of smell is not as highly developed as a dog's. Smaller size, however, by no means signifies that a cat's nose is of less importance to its owner. Encounters with other cats or with unfamiliar people always start

off with extensive sniffing. Unfamiliar objects are also subjected to a thorough olfactory inspection; food is tasted after it has been first tested by smell. In the social life of cats, smells play a particularly important role in communication (see the chapter "Understanding and Misunderstanding," as well as the chapter "At Home and on the Road").

The mucous membrane on the inside of the cat's nose contains over two hundred million cells sensitive to smell. (Humans have only one-tenth of that amount at their disposal!)

Related to the olfactory cells in the nose are the taste receptors on the surface of the tongue. Both kinds of cells are stimulated by contact with chemical substances. While the olfactory cells react to scents in the air, the taste receptors register chemical substances dissolved in saliva or water. The cat has yet another organ, however—which is absent in humans—whose function lies somewhere between smelling and tasting: the Jacobson's organ. It is located in the roof of the mouth between the pharynx and the nasal cavity and consists of a pair of pocketlike closed tubes lined with a kind of olfactory mucous membrane. These "smelling tubes" are connected to the oral cavity through a small opening in the roof of the mouth, right behind the incisors. The cat picks up scent substances out of the air with its tongue and presses them into the orifice of the Jacobson's organ. If it wants to "taste" a scent particularly intensely, often in relation to sexual interests but also to scent traces of urine or catnip, then its tongue just doesn't do the job fast enough. With a half-open mouth and lips slightly pulled back, it "sucks" the scent-filled air into this organ. This flehmen response—which we also see in other mammals, especially hoofed animals—puts a glassy-eyed, slightly stupid grin on the cat's face.

### The "Sixth Sense"

Considering the many feats cats perform, we can only be amazed. When asked for a plausible explanation, we simply have to pass. The cat's precise feeling for time is known to every cat owner. How or by what means the cat measures time we don't know. And about its absolutely incredible homing instinct we can only make suppositions. Actually, an ingenious series of experiments

**When leaping, the tail is simultaneously both a balancing rod and a steering rudder.**

has shown that, in general, the feline sense of direction rapidly diminishes at a distance of seven miles (twelve kilometers), yet again and again completely credible reports reach us of cats that have found their way back home over distances of sixty miles (one hundred kilometers) or more. Whether they orient themselves on their journeys by the changing position of the sun or by constellations or by the geomagnetic fields of the earth, we don't know. In the latter case we would have to accept a special "magnetic sense" in cats. But where does such a sense lie in the body?

Supernatural abilities are often ascribed to the cat. Feats or behavior that couldn't be explained any other way were accepted as proof that cats just had a sixth sense with which they could read the thoughts of humans—or even foresee the future. Of course, cats do not have to bother with parapsychology, they just bring their normal senses to bear. As these are much keener than ours, we often can't comprehend all that cats are aware of. Cats are tremendously keen observers. Let's say, for example, you are sitting in a chair thinking, "I really should feed the cat now." At that very moment, the cat in question jumps up and walks to the empty food bowl in the kitchen. A case of mind reading? Some time before, the cat observed how your posture, during your deliberation, tightened a little,

**Most cats go completely crazy at the smell of catnip (Nepeta cataria).**

and your eyes might inadvertently have strayed toward the kitchen. Since its sense of time had been telling it for quite a while that the habitual dinner hour was fast approaching, it drew the right conclusion—to your great amazement.

The established fact that cats can sense earthquakes well beforehand certainly doesn't come down to supernatural powers either. Possibly the creatures react sensitively to the rapid fluctuations in the earth's magnetic field associated with earthquakes. Or, they may feel the dramatic increase in static electricity in the area in question. Or, they may perceive vibrations of the earth's crust so fine even precise seismological instruments cannot measure them. Maybe this explains the secret of the feline early-warning system.

**ABOVE: The sense of smell plays an important role in the social relationships of cats. Here, a cat is "tasting" with its nose a spot where, just moments before, another cat had been sitting. The smell of urine and the secretions of the anal glands say a lot to interested parties about the rank, gender, and sexual readiness of others of their species.**

**CENTER: The nasal speculum of a cat is hairless and, in a healthy animal, slightly moist. Pigmentation can be rosy or black. Rows of dots on the sides of the upper lip delineate the base of the whiskers.**

**BELOW: Off in open country, cats have managed astonishing feats of orientation when it comes to finding their way home again. Within the familiar range, their excellent memories certainly help; however, we still don't know by what means and in what manner they orient themselves in unfamiliar surroundings.**

# CATS AND PEOPLE

In forests and steppes, and deserts and marshes over half the world, cats lived as perfect hunters of mice and rats. Then humans walked into their lives and cats became domestic pets. In early times, people also selected cats as decoration for their homes. They made use of their talents and brought them, on board their ships, to the other half of the world as well.

No other house pets are by nature as paradoxical as cats. Outstandingly domestic as live-in companions, affectionate and sensitive as friends, cats still stand with two paws in the wild. Their voluntary association with people, along with their outspoken independence, make them perpetual enigmas to us, even though we've been in contact with cats for a very long time (or they with us). In the course of history, the cat has fulfilled varied functions: goddess, mouser, and luxury object.

## From Wildcat to Domestic Cat

People have always tamed wild animals either to make use of their strength and special skills, or merely to have as agreeable live-in companions. A single wild animal that has been tamed and has become accustomed to people is still a far cry from being a pet. A wild animal is domesticated, that is to say, made into a domestic animal or pet, only after it has been bred and raised

**Child and kitten build a close living bond. Play makes up a good part of their day. Both of them not only exercise their agility but also become acquainted with their playing partner's needs and personality.**

# CATS AND PEOPLE

**Most of the other domestic animals had been in the service of humans for thousands of years by the time the cat joined their ranks. Whether they joined up with people voluntarily or whether they were captured, tamed, and bred by people, we don't know. The chart illustrates the probable time in human history various farm animals and pets were domesticated.**

**RIGHT: The Abyssinian cat closely approximates the North African Lybian wildcat, or Kaffir cat, the original form of the earliest domestic cats.**

by people for generations. As a rule, these animals are selectively bred to enhance certain characteristics, thereby increasing their usefulness to people.

How did this process affect the cat? Bones found in excavations in the Middle Eastern oasis city of Jericho verify that cats were already around in the sixth century B.C. Equally old are several small figurines found in the highlands of Anatolia (Hacilar, Turkey). They illustrate women playing with cats. Whether these were true house cats, however, is questionable.

An Egyptian drawing dating from 3000 B.C. depicts a cat wearing a collar. Even in this case, however, it is not

clear whether this was a single animal kept in captivity or a domesticated house cat. At that time, it was a favorite Egyptian pastime to tame and keep wild animals. Tame baboons, hyenas, lions, mongooses, and even crocodiles used to romp around their houses. Why would they make an exception for any wild cat, especially one that allows itself to be tamed relatively easily? From approximately 1600 B.C. on, increasing numbers of inscriptions, drawings, paintings, and statues of cats are to be found all over Egypt, so we can safely assume that, by this time at least, the cat was truly becoming a house pet. It remains unclear whether cats voluntarily

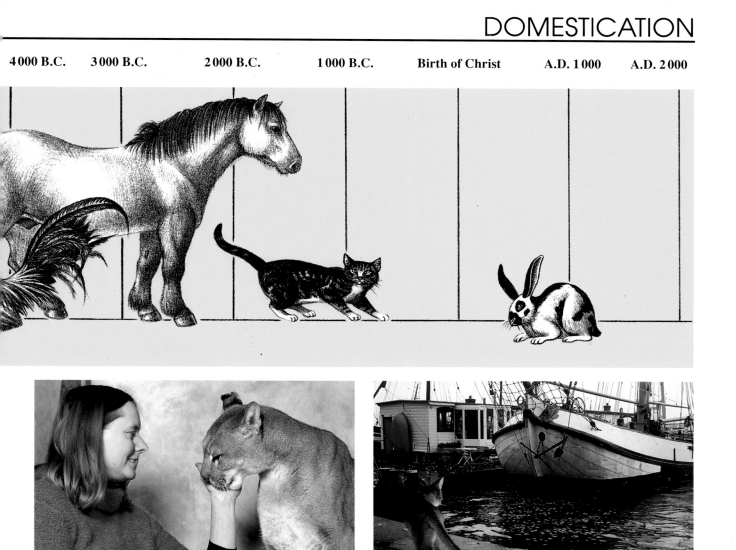

| 4000 B.C. | 3000 B.C. | 2000 B.C. | 1000 B.C. | Birth of Christ | A.D. 1000 | A.D. 2000 |

cast their lot in with people because they conveniently found prey in abundance near human food stores (ever since people had abandoned the nomadic way of life to pursue agriculture they had been building storage bins for grain where mice and rats were plentiful), or whether people captured cats in the wild and then brought them into their settlements for the purpose of mousing. Looking back, we probably won't be able to answer this question with any certainty.

**Animals tamed from the wild like this puma (LEFT) are not pets by a long shot. A variety of animal can be considered domesticated only when it has been kept and raised by humans for many generations.**

**For hundreds of years, the ship's cat was an important crew member whose role was to prevent voracious rodents from laying into the ship's provender on long sea voyages.**

Catching mice and rats, that was the first "job" people gave cats in the course of their domestication, and through the present time this has remained the main task of farm cats.

We are familiar with depictions of cats mainly from ancient Egypt, but also from Asia Minor. This is a reproduction.

### The Domestic Cat's Wild Ancestors

The ancestors to our domestic cats can be found among Old World wildcats, who have the scientific name *Felis silvestris*. This species of small cat is widespread and is represented in various regional subspecies. One of these is the Lybian wildcat or the Kaffir cat (*Felis silvestris lybica*), which used to be native to all of North Africa. It is certain that the first domestic cats of the ancient Egyptians descended from them. As domestic cats proliferated throughout the world, it is possible that still other wildcat subspecies contributed to their genetic heritage. The long-haired and dark European wildcat (*Felis silvestris silvestris*) might

have had a part to play, as might varieties of Asian desert wildcat (*Felis silvestris ornata*) inhabiting the steppes. The influence of the latter, however, was certainly not large, if it existed at all. European wildcats are extraordinarily shy creatures that remain markedly unapproachable as adults, even when reared by hand. In contrast, the wildcats belonging to the African subspecies are virtually born pets. As kittens caught in the wild, Kaffir cats lose their shyness after a few days and adapt themselves quickly to life in human society.

### The Spread of the Domestic Cat

While a religious cat cult, which elevated the cat to the rank of goddess, was developing in Egypt (see the chap-

Whether the models for the first Egyptian statues were already domesticated is questionable.

All cultures have ascribed, and continue to ascribe, predominantly female characteristics to cats. Affectionate pleasure-seekers with minds of their own, cats are symbols of sensuality and sexuality. (Eighteenth-century oil painting by François Boucher.)

ter "Religion and Art"), news of the usefulness of domestic cats in controlling rodents spread beyond Egypt's borders. Seafaring Phoenician merchants—via their ships—were primarily responsible for the spread of the mouser all around the Mediterranean. After all, people everywhere were suffering from plagues of voracious rodents that consumed their grain and other food stores. The first cats arrived on the Greek mainland no later than 500 B.C. The Greeks immediately brought them to southern Italy. The Romans, in turn, must have been responsible for the further spread of the domestic cat to northern Europe. At the same time, cats sailed on board trading vessels to the east as well. They reached India in approximately 200 B.C., and from there they spread into the Far East and China.

## Mousers by Trade

Humans offer domestic cats roofs over their heads; soft, warm places to sleep; and regularly filled bowls of food (or at least the opportunity to find generous amounts of food on the side). Still, many people also expect cats to perform services in return. Two primary tasks are generally assigned cats: They should catch mice and rats, and be endearing companions. First, we will in-

Cats were most honored in the advanced civilization of Egypt—as godly forms, totemic creatures, and temple cats.

Today in Egyptian souvenir shops cats, or rather statues of Bastet, are sold to tourists.

vestigate their function as mousers, which is still the foremost function of farm cats, even today. Ever since people settled and engaged in farming, they have had to defend their food stores from rodents. From the earliest times, people have taken into their homes animals they knew had a predilection for eating mice. In the Mediterranean region, the animals of choice were mongooses or (nonpoisonous) snakes; in cooler central Europe the selection fell on ferrets (which nowadays are popular pets in the United States). Once cats began their victorious migra-

# CATS AND PEOPLE

Today, in an era in which cats do not first and foremost have to make themselves useful but rather just "pretty" or decorative, purebred cats are going through a boom.

The Turkish Van, now simply called Turkish cat (ABOVE), is a very old breed. Its home is the mountain region around Van Lake in Turkey. This breed first came to Europe in the 1960s. The unusual characteristic of this breed is that many of these cats will voluntarily enter the water and swim.

Although the Burmese (CENTER) is a relatively recent breed, it probably traces its origins to a very old type of cat from Southeast Asia. In 1930 an American brought a dark brown cat to the United States from Rangoon and mated it with a Siamese tom. From this union a new breed was born: the Burmese cat.

It is a similar story with the Singapore (BELOW). Who knows for how long this delicate little breed had been at home in the streets of Singapore? It was entirely unknown to the Western world until 1975, when the first of these feline firecrackers was imported to California. Enthusiasts continued to breed it and thus created a new breed recognized by breeding associations.

tion across Europe, the other animals soon lost their jobs. As mousers, cats were simply more successful than all the others. And for centuries a farmer considered himself lucky if he had a cat to call his own.

Another "job market" soon opened up for cats on the big sailing vessels that were beginning to ply the oceans. The ship's cat was as much a crew member as the cook or the cabin boy. In German there exists even today the word "catwalk," which in that language means gangplank, a narrow board that serves as a link between ship and land. On board ships, cats reached the remotest parts of the world.

Even today many cats still "work" to earn their keep. In England, cats are kept in most of the big administration and office buildings and fed by the personnel in return for their mousing services. Cats shouldn't be starved in order to encourage them to catch mice. Feeding them additional food encourages them to perform their work closer to home (see also the chapter "The Hunter and the Hunted").

## From Common Cat to Pedigreed Purebred

In the colorful history of its life with humans, the cat has survived heady heights and the most abysmal depths, from Egyptian deification to medieval condemnation and burning as a witch's familiar. At last, with the spirit of modern times, came the reinstatement of its reputation, which is still recovering today. The Baroque bourgeoisie came up with the idea of using the cat as an accessory for salons and a fondling creature for the ladies. Soon the "common" cat was too common for this purpose. People longed for nobler specimens. The time of purebred cat had come. Reports of long-haired cats inhabiting the Persian province of Chorasmia first reached Europe in the seventeenth century. Through a mutation—an accidental alteration of hereditary material that occurs regularly in nature—the domestic cat had been granted a long, silky coat. In Europe these "Persian" cats were initially known as "Angoras."

Modern, systematic cat breeding, as it is now pursued by numerous breeders, was first practiced a good hundred and fifty years ago. England became the stronghold of purebred cat breeding. In 1871 the first cat show in the world was held in London, where one could already admire a few "Siamese." They were still recent imports to Europe, although the gene mutation leading to the typical coloration pattern had probably occurred around A.D. 1500 in Southeast Asia. At any rate, precise descriptions from Ayudha, the then-capital of the kingdom of Siam (present-day Thailand) originate from this time. The primary effect of this so-called Siamese mutation is the reduction in the dark pigment in the hair and eyes. In addition, the amount of pigment that can be produced is dependent on temperature. The lower the temperature, the more pigment is produced. As face and ears, paws and tail on a cat are always a little

**The Siamese is a demonstrably venerable breed. An ancient manuscript was found in Thailand (formerly Siam) in which there is a precise description of this light-colored cat with the dark "insignia" on its head, paws, and tail.**

**The Maine Coon is the giant among pedigreed cats (LEFT). The tom occasionally manages to reach a strapping twenty pounds (nine kilograms).**

**Another big, powerfully built cat is the Norwegian wildcat (CENTER). Its long coat is extremely water resistant; its thick undercoat ensures that the cold, wet weather of northern Europe doesn't bother it much.**

**The Persian cat (RIGHT) didn't become the most bred and most often kept long-haired cat yesterday. Opinions on its beauty are pretty controversial. One thing is certain, though: The Persian certainly can't be described as a temperamental handful.**

cooler than the body, dark hairs will grow in these places on a Siamese. Siamese cats that stay predominantly in the open air have a darker overall coloring than indoor Siamese.

## Purebred According to the Book

Enthusiasts and breeders of pedigreed cats soon formed clubs and associations so they could jointly indulge in their common hobby. From these early beginnings emerged today's blossoming of organizations devoted to the breeding of felines. Under their auspices, experiences are exchanged, shows organized, pedigrees written up, studbooks maintained, and breed features established. In the United States, one such organization is the Purebred Catbreeders Society. In Europe, the international umbrella organization of cat breeding as-

sociations, called or FIFe for Fédération Internationale Féline d'Europe (which recently lowercased the E at the end of its acronym when it accepted non-European associations into its membership and therefore dropped the word Europe from its name to become the Fédération Internationale Féline), worked up standards for all the cat breeds it recognized. For the neophyte cat lover these detailed descriptions of the ideal within some particular breed of cat sound pretty fussy. Not only are the structure and shape of the head, the coloration and texture of the coat minutely stipulated, but so are the color of the eyes, whether there are hairs on the insides of the ears, the breadth of the space between the ears, and so forth. Breeders do their best to conform their cats to these rules. Only a "flawless" animal will be recognized by the breeders' association and re-

ceive a pedigree—and only then will it be valuable. With the estimated value of pedigreed cats on the rise, cat breeding has become quite a lucrative business.

Since the turn of the century, numerous new breeds have been created from the first varieties of domestic cat: the Angora, the Siamese, and common short-hair. The long-haired Angora provided the foundation for the present-day Persian, which has a much stockier build and has consequently become round, soft, and cherublike in appearance. (Even today, the original Angora cats—along with the somewhat shorter-haired Van, now called Turkish—are still being bred true to the prototype Persian, especially in Turkey.) Crosses between Persians and Siamese cats have produced the long-haired Birman cat.

Until now the cat has stubbornly resisted breeding attempts to give it an essentially different body structure. Unlike the results of dog breeding, which led to the different shapes of the Pekinese, dachshund, greyhound, and St. Bernard, the results of breeding cats confine themselves, by and large, to variations in color, length, and texture of the coat. The size and weight of various cat breeds vary within limited parameters. The United States, the land of superlatives, holds the cat size record with the Maine Coon: The tom of this magnificent, long-haired breed tips the scales at between fifteen and twenty pounds (seven to nine kilograms), roughly twice the weight of a small everyday house cat.

Havana brown, Burmese, Somali, Balinese, Egyptian Mau, Abyssinian, and whatever else modern pedigreed cats are called nowadays, they all originated in the little nesting baskets of European and American breeders, no matter how exotic their names may sound.

The elegant, dark brown Havana is intentionally "bred out" from dark Siamese and brown or black short-hairs.

Persian cats (ABOVE) come with all possible colors of fur and eyes. The different varieties have been carefully classified by breeders' associations and assigned numbers.

As far as the typical Persian's face is concerned, breeders' ambitions know no limits. They should be rounder and rounder; their noses shorter and shorter. Particularly extreme types are called "Peke-faced" Persians (ABOVE RIGHT). Their skulls are so deformed that the animals have trouble using their teeth properly and frequently suffer from breathing problems.

## Excesses in Breeding

In recent times, endeavors at breeding increasingly innovative feline varieties have led to some pretty peculiar results. Animals that used to be removed from litters as failures are suddenly being pampered and used for further breeding. If only they would pass on their special features on a predictable basis! Whether the new breeds created in this way are wonderfully beautiful or not is beside the point. Matters of taste can't be argued anyway. And insofar as the new cat is hale and hearty enough to live the way of cats, there is nothing at all to be said against these breeds. Unfortunately, this isn't true in all cases.

For instance, the Manx cat, the tailless native of the British Isle of Man, came about through a gene mutation as a result of extreme inbreeding. Their taillessness goes hand-in-hand with a whole array of extremely negative characteristics. Their hindquarters are carried by legs that are too long. This lends the Manx cat

a hobbling gait reminiscent of a rabbit rather than a graceful cat, and causes it considerable trouble when jumping down off things. A deformed pelvis and poor formation of the anal sphincter hinder it when responding to the call of nature. These disorders extend from chronic constipation to an absolute inability to retain urine and excrement. In breeding, stillbirths occur very frequently, or else inviable kittens are born that die after a few days. It is absolutely incomprehensible how such a zoologically torturous abnormality ever became a standard breed. In this case, however, the breeders aren't the only ones at fault. Unhappily, the tailless cats of the Isle of Man have become an exceptional tourist attraction, and tourists do want to have them. The few breeders can't even satisfy present demands and boast waiting lists several years long.

Persian cats, according to breeding ideals, should be as round as possible. The Persian's profile is extremely foreshortened. Its nose, which can barely be described as a little stub, appears as if it were simply flattened. Yet, for many breeders, it still isn't flat enough. With extreme "super Persians," so-called Peke-faced Persians, the deformations of the skull considerably impair the animals' health and wellbeing. The frequent over- and underbite caused by the jaw anomaly make these cats useless at catching prey, and mother cats can't chew off the umbilical cords of their kittens by themselves. Their tear ducts have become so short, the fluid cannot drain away through the normal channels inside the eye. This leads to permanently runny eyes. With particularly extreme types, their little noses are so badly malformed that the animals have to cope with breathing problems.

There is one other inherited abnormality that should be mentioned, one that is also common in dogs and laboratory mice and rats: hairlessness. Among cats, this degeneration has been found in Siamese cats. Hairless Siamese cats are called Sphynx cats in the United States and have actually been elected to their own breed. The fact that these skinny, wrinkly creatures are more reminiscent of the extraterrestrial E. T. than of elegant, svelte cats doesn't seem to bother their breeders. Bald cats are extraordinarily delicate charges and prone to all manner of illness. They lack any covering for warmth. Besides this, it seems that the gene

**One of the most recent "creations" of cat breeders is the Poodle cat. It has the crimped fur of the Rex combined with the drop ears of the Scottish Fold (RIGHT). The combination Siamese and Scottish Fold (LEFT) likewise yields a breed for people who want to keep a cat—but preferably one that doesn't look like a cat!**

**The little cocked ears of the Scottish Fold make it easy to recognize. It is difficult to breed true as the hereditary factor for drop ears threatens a frequency of inviable kittens and stillbirths. That's why it is always crossed with normal-eared animals. This cross breeding, and the fact that the hereditary factor for drop ears is not dominant, means that both ear types are generally to be found in litters—as these two four-week-old littermates (FAR LEFT) demonstrate.**

**Children don't just love to play with cats, they are also all too willing to snuggle with them. You can certainly turn a blind eye when a child shares its bed with a healthy, well-tended cat.**

**Cats don't like being clumsily handled or roughly picked up. Even if they tolerate it for a little while, sooner or later they will try to wriggle out of a hold or defend themselves. (Children who are still all thumbs shouldn't be left to play with cats unsupervised.) However, as soon as a child has learned to respect a cat's needs, nothing stands in the way of their being great pals.**

for hairlessness is coupled with a so-called lethal factor, which means that litters will always include a lot of stillbirths or inviable kittens.

Compared with these truly miserable creatures, droopy ears or curly hair are the results of harmless breeding games. The Scottish Fold may look relatively remarkable for a cat, but since the cat itself likely doesn't know this, it leads a completely unencumbered feline life. Its fellow cats seem able to distinguish the little floppy ears from ears belligerently flattened, and in mixed groups things are no more or less aggressive or congenial than in a group of cats with only normal ears. The Rex—whose curly fur is absolutely atypical for cats and gives the impression of being freshly crimped, especially on the back—is a lively feline. Mu-

tations that led to these splendid locks have appeared repeatedly and independently in England, Germany, and the United States since the 1950s and were immediately "stabilized" into new breeds. Incidentally, these cats were named after the Rex rabbits that have a similarly curly coat.

All purebred cats have one thing in common, and that is they have little chance of surviving into old age in the wild or independently of humans as strays. They have become utterly human creations and rely on human care. Shut up indoors for generation after generation, they know only in their collective memory what hunting is all about. It seems 80 to 85 percent of all domestic cats living with us are, however, still totally ordinary "common cats" with no pedigree, but with a good dose of indepen-

dence and amazingly unadulterated instincts instead. They are the ones this book is all about and what is meant first and foremost when discussing "the cat."

## The Influence of Cats on People

Everyday life without cats is unthinkable. We encounter them in product advertising, in cartoons, in the movies, or in the form of bric-a-brac, jewelry, or in the designs of basic commodities. They may cross our paths in a suburban development or somewhere on vacation. Even in our everyday speech the cat has its niche. If someone's shy, we ask if "the cat's got your tongue." If someone's the opposite,

A cat makes a wonderful playmate who provides a lot of stick-to-itness and patience—but only if the cat is willing. A child also has to have a healthy dose of self-awareness to be able to respect an occasional refusal or rejection from the cat without being disappointed.

It can mean a lot to children to take care of a cat all by themselves. They have a real job to learn, taking responsibility for a weaker family member.

someone who looks like "the cat that swallowed the canary," they may "let the cat out of the bag" and inadvertently make someone else feel like they're "a cat on hot bricks." But, in the end, "all cats are gray in the dark," and speaking of dark, "it's time to wind the cat and put out the clock."

At least 30 percent of American households accommodate one or more couch cougars. Although a higher percentage of households have dogs, the total number of cats kept as pets is higher. Based on the statistics, cat owners tend to keep more than one feline companion. Nevertheless, not everyone is a cat lover. Some people don't want to have anything to do with cats, because you can't control cats easily or train them to become unquestioningly obedient like dogs. Others have an outright fear of cats, particularly of black

# CATS AND PEOPLE

cats. It seems that the medieval notion of evil hidden in the form of a cat still exists somewhere. The irrational fear of cats can even take on morbid proportions. Such people, suffering from ailurophobia, as it is called, break out in a cold sweat at the mere sight of a cat, and they then begin to tremble. Well-known ailurophobes include Julius Caesar and Napoleon, neither of whom could be described as a particularly sensitive or tolerant leader.

## Children and Cats

Konrad Lorenz, the great mentor of behaviorism, once wrote: "The pet's position [in the household] is seriously growing as a factor in raising children. It is growing in its measure of significance in that an urbanized humanity is alienating itself from nature." Perhaps the wish so many children have to own a pet springs from an instinctive search for an opportunity to establish con-

tact with nature. It is certain that people who, as children, were able to have good, long-standing experiences with cats and other animals will also readily surround themselves with animals when they are adults. In the company of cats, children can learn a lot that will leave its mark, not only on how they relate to animals but also on how they approach life in general. They learn, above all, to respect the will of a partner. A cat can be an enthusiastic, as well as patient, play-

**At a time when the number of single-person households keeps rising, increasing numbers of men are turning to cats. They value their gentle housemates, who wait patiently for them to come back from work in the evening.**

mate for a child, but only as long as it is willing. The claws of an unwilling cat speak a language that every child understands, literally, at one fell swoop. An older child can also be entrusted with the task of feeding and tending a cat. Through this, the child learns to recognize the needs of others and to bear responsibility for a weaker member of the family.

## Cats as Signficant Others

The cliché of the cat being the typical pet of single, older women is less and less apt today. Since the number of single-person households in our society is rapidly on the rise, the cat has taken over a new role and become the "singles' animal." A residence where one expects to find a cat on returning home from work isn't an empty house. This is something that is appreciated by more and more young people. The cat one lives with brings joy into the home, steering people away from their worries, problems, and afflictions.

There is hardly any scientific research on how people and cats relate, and few reports are actually backed by statistics. It is only in the past twenty years that doctors and psychologists have been interested in the pleasant and, depending on the circum-

stances, even therapeutic effect of relating to animals. This much has come to light: When you stroke a contented cat curled up in your lap, your blood pressure drops and tense muscles loosen up. Body and soul relax. A long-term American study from the 1980s in which seniors were "prescribed" cats as companions showed a positive effect in all cases on the health of the test subjects, providing they had established a sincere emotional bond with their cat. These people were less depressed and sickly, their blood pressure became normalized, and in some cases, even the blood sugar level of diabetics dropped.

But, a relationship always takes two, and if it is to be a good relationship, the two have to be well matched. This goes for both cats and cat owners. In a wide-ranging study, the characters of various people and cats were "paired off," and then the couple was observed over an extended period of time to see how they got along together. The figures verified what had been supposed for a long time: People with a lack of self-awareness have great difficulty becoming friendly with shy, fearful, or even timid cats. Such cats quickly withdraw and hide. This can leave insecure people with the feeling they are being rejected. In contrast, even shy cats are safe with loving, tolerant people who are at peace with themselves. A cat that is friendly to people, that keeps taking the initiative to

make contact of its own accord, and that comes close and snuggles up can, on the other hand, be an excellent therapy for people suffering from mild to moderately severe depression. Cats are being kept intentionally by more and more rest homes, rehabilitation centers, and care facilities. Animal-facilitated therapy is the professional term. It corresponds to an age-old life experience: Together with a friend, one goes through life better and overcomes difficult situations more easily. And cats can be extraordinarily good friends!

**A cat imparts that nice feeling of being needed, especially to older, single people. And when the little grandchild also comes to visit, Gramma knows how to form a bridge between the child and the animal.**

**For many young women a cat is certainly, consciously or unconsciously, a kind of substitute child. Independent and hardworking, the modern woman stands on her own two feet, and yet at the same time she would like to mother and be affectionate to a sweet little being—just the role for a cat.**

# CAT BEHAVIOR

# BIRTH AND RAISING

Born blind and helpless, newborn kittens are entirely dependent for their care on their mother—at least for the time being. Most female cats are devoted mothers. When they have to, they can also turn into hellcats to defend their young. Kittens learn from their mother whatever they will need in their future cat-life. At the age of about a half year, for free-ranging cats, the young are at last so self-sufficient that the intimate bond between mother and kittens gradually dissolves. Indoor cats, which are cared for by humans, can live in-dependently of their mother as soon as they are weaned.

t is early in the year and time for feline love. Cats' courtship songs echo far and wide through the night. The mating instinct inevitably brings the female and tom together. And, as nature would have it, such an amorous adventure is not without its consequences: The female becomes pregnant.

Stimulated by the sex act, the female ovulates about twenty-four to thirty-six hours after mating (or several couplings). Usually several eggs are released by the ovaries and fertilized, for in the end kittens are to be born. Some of the still-minute embryos die and are reabsorbed by the mother. This is completely normal for cats and takes place without any externally detectable signs.

If the female mates with different toms, one after another (see the chapter "Lust and Love")—which is quite often the case when there is no acute shortage of toms in the vicinity—sheer chance decides whose sperm will win the race and fertilize the eggs. This means, of course, that the kittens of a single litter may have different fathers.

## Gestation

For the first three to four weeks you cannot tell anything about the cat's condition. Most likely you will notice that she has suddenly become extremely home-loving, only seldom wandering around outside for long and staying close to home. Many cats now seem to have an increased need for sleep—at least they often

**To carry her young, the mother sets her teeth carefully, but firmly, in the kitten's neck. As soon as she takes hold, the kitten exhibits the "limp response" by means of a reflex arc.**

# BIRTH AND RAISING

hardly get up from their favorite spots. Usually they are also more devoted to their human family than before, constantly wanting to cuddle and snuggle. In the fourth week, the teats start to become a darker pink and protrude more noticeably. During the fifth week, you can see the bellies of some cats gradually getting rounder. (You would be hard pressed to see this with long-haired cats, mind you. Generally, they can keep their condition a secret longer.) Some cats have huge bellies toward the end of their term, especially when they are carrying many young; in others, hardly any change can be seen until delivery, so you wonder where these cat-mothers manage to hide their unborn kittens.

As a rule, the period of gestation for house cats lasts between sixty-two and sixty-five days, although, as with people, a certain divergence above or below this time frame is absolutely normal: Occasionally the term ends in as short as fifty-nine days, and sometimes a cat won't throw her litter before the seventieth or seventy-second day.

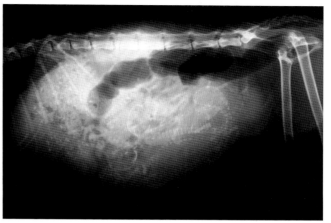

## The Nesting Site

One to two weeks before the delivery date the cat starts looking around for a suitable place for a nesting site. It should be dark, warm, and protected from drafts. Most often a cat finds itself a peaceful corner where few disturbances are to be expected. However, a cat close to her human family can also set up her nursery in the middle of the living room to make sure she isn't shut off from family life during the time of her motherhood. A soft layer of bedding is a good idea. If necessary the cat will do without, but it makes everything easier.

Should the nesting site selected by her well-meaning human friends correspond to what the female herself has in mind, she accepts this service gladly. If not, she simply ignores the box or basket and instead seek a place that is more appealing to her. She

will find, as cats always have, a suitable niche in which to raise her young. The variations range from a drawer in a commode to a bookshelf, from a pile of sweaters on a shelf in the closet to the hollow under a blanket. Farm cats prefer dark corners in the hay lofts of barns; feral cats seek out thick undergrowth, tree hollows, old sheds, or cellars.

## What's the right way to treat a pregnant cat?

Pregnancy is neither an illness nor an affliction, but the most natural thing in the world. Above all, you shouldn't give the cat extra helpings, one after another, because the same rule applies here as for expectant human mothers: Excessive increase in weight during pregnancy burdens the organism and can lead to stress on the organs. Veterinarians currently recommend feeding pregnant cats a balanced, high-protein kitten food with calcium and phosphorous. Usually a cat puts on two to three pounds (one to one and one-half kilograms) of body weight up to the moment of giving birth, depending on her initial weight and the number of young she is carrying. With advanced pregnancy, the internal relationships are pretty cramped anyway, so dividing the daily food rations into several smaller portions to be eaten throughout the day, rather than serving two large portions, is recommended.

**A frankly pregnant female cat prefers to lie comfortably on her side (FAR LEFT). Maternal instincts are not initially aroused at the birth of the young, but surface a few days prior to giving birth. Sometimes other adult cats benefit from this and are diligently licked (CENTER LEFT).**

**Some time before term the expectant mother seeks out a suitable place for her nesting site. Drawers or clothes shelves are among the desirable accommodations (CENTER RIGHT).**

**With the aid of an X-ray after the forty-second to fifty-second day of gestation (any earlier might be damaging to the kittens), the veterinarian can confirm pregnancy beyond doubt and also the number of kittens to be expected. Here there are three unborn kittens (FAR RIGHT).**

**The ideal nest for the litter is big enough that the female can stretch out completely. By extensive "trial lays" the suitability of the nest is thoroughly examined.**

**When, after powerful expulsing contractions, the head or (as here) hindquarters of the kitten become visible at the vaginal opening, the birth is only a few minutes away. With a final strain, the young kitten presents itself. It is still wrapped in the fetal membrane, which the mother tears off with her teeth to free the little one. After that, the cat works the little body over with powerful strokes of her tongue. This is not only cleansing, but the massage stimulates both the breathing and the circulation of the newborn.**

## The Birth

About twelve to twenty-four hours before the birth, most female cats become noticeably restless. Again and again, they visit the selected nesting place and paw the bedding into shape. At this point they won't eat anything. At first the contractions obviously resemble the urge to defecate, as inexperienced cats often look for their litter box or a suitable place outside. A light discharge of amniotic fluid from the genital tract opening is the first recognizable sign that the onset of labor is near at hand. Contractions become stronger and occur at shorter and shorter intervals. Depending on her character, the female will bear them silently, groan softly, or meow loudly and plaintively.

In general, the behavior of females in this phase differs widely. Inexperienced cats, or those with a strong human fixation, absolutely don't want to be left alone during these difficult hours. Most cats, however, especially mothers who have had a number of litters, withdraw to be undisturbed during labor and birth. The majority of cat births take place during the night and in absolute quiet.

The cat stays in her nesting site for longer periods of time. Between contractions she licks her vaginal opening forcefully. This is not only cleansing; the main reason she does this is to massage and loosen up the tissue. It will then dilate more easily during birth, lessening the danger that the vaginal walls will tear.

The contractions up till now have served to open the cervix and to the widen the uterus. Now expulsive contractions set in. The cat lies on her side or squats as if to defecate. She uses her stomach muscles to assist the contractions. Suddenly everything goes very fast: the first kitten presents. Most kittens are born headfirst, but almost a third enter the world hindquarters first, which, as a

**Isn't he cute? In only a few days, this little kitten will be gazing at the world with wide-eyed curiosity.**

rule, does not present any complications for cats. After a couple of minutes at most, the little wet bundle is lying beside the mother in the nest. If the amniotic sac hasn't already broken, the female will now tear it off to release the kitten. She will lick up the amniotic fluid and eat the membrane. Then she will immediately start licking her kitten. This powerful tongue massage not only cleans and dries the kitten, it is especially important to stimulate the newborn's circulation and respiration.

Finally, the afterbirth, or placenta, is either discharged or the mother pulls it out using the umbilical cord. The female eats the placenta complete with cord. If it hasn't already come off, she now nibbles the kitten free of the umbilical cord, biting through the cord about an inch (two to three centimeters) from its stomach. With most mammals, after the exertions of the delivery, the mother eats the afterbirth. Cats are no exception. This behavior has various important functions. For one, the nest is kept clean and thereby the risk of infection is reduced; for another, it gets rid of smells that could easily

**Finally the afterbirth is expelled and eaten, usually right away, by the mother. While the baby kitten finds the source of milk and sucks in its first meal, its mother is still diligently licking it completely clean and dry.**

59

alert a predator to the newborn's presence. In keeping with these hygienic measures, the mother also licks the amniotic fluid from the bedding of the nest as best she can. An added benefit is that the afterbirth provides a high-quality food for the mother cat in the form of a concentrated dose of nutrients.

**Most cats are devoted mothers. Relentlessly they lick their young so their fur always stays velvety soft and sparkling clean. At the same time, this is a healthy body massage for the little ones and also firms the social bond between mother and infant.**

It might be only a few minutes—or several hours could pass—before renewed contractions set in and the second kitten is born. The pattern repeats itself until the entire litter lies between the legs of the mother.

## The Brand-New Mother

Once all the kittens have been born and are well taken care of, the mother cat finally allows herself a rest. She licks herself thoroughly and then lies down, relaxing on her side. Her body forms a half-circle around the little ones that press into her belly, her legs lightly enclose her young. A deep, contented purring emanates from the female's throat, while the newborns suckle on her teats for the first time.

The first milk the mother provides is called colostrum. It is extremely important for the baby kittens as it is particularly rich in nutrients and, moreover, contains antibodies that confer an effective protection against infection.

Again and again the female works over her young with her tongue. As she licks each little belly and anus, elimination is stimulated. Without the maternal tongue massage this process would never get underway in the little ones! To keep the nest clean, the female meticulously licks up the kittens' excrement until they can take care of their "business" outside the nest.

For the first few days after the birth, the mother barely leaves the nest. At most, after the little ones have let go of her teats and contentedly fallen asleep, she trots off to use her toilet and, if she has family accommodations, to peek at her food bowl in passing. The first couple of days she won't go hunting as it would take too long. Some cats don't eat at all, or only very little, during this time, even when ample food is placed right under their noses.

It is not unusual for a mother cat to decide, a couple of days after the birth, to settle her entire litter in another nest, even when there has been absolutely no disturbance of the birthing site. She is responding to an instinct that has remained with her since ancient times before she became a protected house pet. Feral cats often remove their young from the place of their birth, probably because the scent of the blood and amniotic fluid that escaped during birth might attract predators.

Multicolored litters like this are common among cats. The inheriting of fur color follows highly complicated rules, and when some tomcat or other from the neighborhood—or maybe several—had access, it is even more complex. As soon as the young are hanging on the teats suckling with relish in the security of the nest, almost every mother cat will let out a deep, satisfied purring. Each of the baby kittens develops a definite preference for a specific teat early on and will defend this suckling place stubbornly from siblings who also want to try it out every once in a while. While suckling, little front paws rhythmically "knead" the mother's stomach. This kneading is innate to kittens. They use it to massage the tissue of the mother's mammary gland ridge to stimulate the flow of milk.

Besides drinking, sleeping is the main activity for infant kittens during the first part of their lives (ABOVE LEFT). However, even the littlest ones make every effort to raise their heads and hoist themselves up on their thin little legs (ABOVE RIGHT).

At the age of four weeks, the curiosity of young kittens is already limitless. The radius of their excursions becomes larger and larger. Actually they don't get too far away from their mother and littermates, but in the enthusiasm of discovery it can happen every once in a while that contact with the family is lost and they find themselves alone—the way it happened to this Persian kitten (BELOW). Instead of wandering around it meows at the top of its lungs for its mother, who hears this cry for help over astonishingly long distances—and immediately hurries over, consoles the little one by licking it, and then guides it back.

## The Newborns

Baby kittens, when they see the first light of day, are as yet "incomplete" little beings. Blind, deaf, toothless, covered with a thin coat of fur, and with legs that are much too weak, they lie in the hollow of the nest. In biology, animals that are helpless to such an extent are described, bluntly and prosaically, as "nest squatters." They are utterly and completely reliant upon the care of their mother, who gives them food,

shelter, and above all, warmth. Warmth is crucial for baby kittens' survival. Thermoregulation in their little bodies is not yet competent, which means they can't maintain a constant body temperature by themselves. Consequently, littermates always nestle very close to one another when they sleep, so they can warm each other. Should a kitten cool down, for instance, because it has fallen or inadvertently scrambled out of the nest, it can easily die. This is why baby kittens let out piercing cries for their mother as soon as they find themselves out of the nest somehow and beginning to get cold. The female can hear this call from a long distance and hurries over to carry her kitten back to the nest. At the age of seven weeks, the kittens' ability to regulate body temperature is as developed as that of adult cats.

## Infancy

A newborn kitten is four to six inches (ten to fifteen centimeters) long and weighs between two and one-half and four and one-half ounces (seventy and 130 grams). It grows rapidly during the first days of its life, essentially just clinging to the milk source. Even though the mother has eight teats to offer, the little ones most often crowd around the hindmost ones.

First, these are more easily accessible and second, they usually provide more milk than the front teats. (In some females the front pair stays completely dry.) Soon each infant kitten has its favorite teat, which it can recognize by smell and which it defends from its littermates more or less energetically. The baby kittens stimulate the flow of milk by kneading the mother's stomach with their little paws.

Between the ninth and twelfth day the kittens open their eyes. The eyelids, which were still tightly knit together at birth, now gradually loosen, although the kittens can't see right away. It takes at least another two to three days before they respond to a light source or movement.

Around the twelfth day their baby teeth appear: first the incisors, then the canines, and finally the molars, in the same fashion as human babies. At the age of six to eight weeks the set of baby teeth is complete.

From their earliest days, the kittens can raise themselves on their front paws and crawl short distances, dragging their fat little bellies on the ground. By the second week, they are already making their first attempts to stand up, to walk, or even to hop.

## The Mother-Child Bond

In contrast with their eyes and ears, the sense of smell in newborn kittens is already well developed. Consequently they get to know their mother first by her personal scent.

**At four weeks the kitten already looks out into the world with a sense of enterprise and excitement. With alert senses, it explores its surroundings. It has so much to learn!**

In their second week of life, the kittens' sense of hearing starts to function. Now they can also get to know their mother through vocal contact. The little ones hear her contented purring when the whole family lies together in the nest and she is suckling them. Then, the world is in order for all of them. They also hear the beckoning crooning of the female as she encourages her young to suckle or announces washing hour. When the kittens are bigger, she uses the same sound to call to them or to invite them to follow her on a walk.

Only when the kittens see the world with open eyes do they experience what their mother and their littermates look like. Now what biologists and psychologists call optical imprinting takes place: Using the image in their memory, the kittens can distinguish their mother from all other cats at a fair distance; at the same time, it is impressed on them what their fellow cats look like. After all, later on in life they will have to know with whom they are disputing over territory and rank, and whom they will court when in the mating mood. Kittens' behavior vis à vis other cats or people isn't exclusively conditioned by the initial sensory impressions of their real (or putative) mother, however. It also depends a good deal on experiences they collect during the first weeks of early kittenhood (see also the chapter "At Home and on the Road").

## The Role of the Father

For cats, raising the young is the mother's responsibility. With feral cats, the tom usually doesn't come anywhere near the nest. Among house cats socially grouped together, each tom behaves very differently. Some toms take note of the young ones by inspecting the nest briefly and ignoring it from then on; others make a large detour around the nest

**A tom living in a domestic setting with the mother cat takes advantage of her brief absence to inspect the nest basket. Although the tom doesn't mean them any harm, the little ones are visibly uneasy with his proximity.**

**Tomcats often feel bothered by the overtures of curious kittens and react with corresponding irritability. As the youngest members of the group, kittens have a low social rank. The tom will show them who's boss—at home, at least!**

just as, later, they avoid the romping kittens; still others assume some kind of a paternal role by regularly cleaning the little ones and playing with them. One tom was even seen bringing food to a nursing female in her nest, behaving like the proverbial provider and devoted family man.

In feral cat groups, the toms are tolerant of and patient with the young. After all, they can't be sure the kittens are not their own. It is quite different, though, when a foreign tom arrives on the scene with the intention of taking on a dominant role in the local cat population. This tom can be absolutely sure he is not the father of any of the kittens. An ancient instinct drives him to spread his own hereditary material as widely as possible by fathering many young. A female who already has young is not ready for mating; however, if she loses her young, she can be in heat again a few weeks later and the new tom will stand a chance. A strange

**To be a mother cat is a thoroughly exhausting job that takes all her time and energy. From the time her young are first born, she is constantly busy cleaning them and grooming their fur. Sometimes the little ones are nothing short of insatiable. A baby kitten who just doesn't want to let a teat go can even be dragged a short distance by a departing mother.**

**Should the nesting place no longer seem safe enough to the mother cat, she relocates her young. With a grip on their necks, she carries them one after another to the new spot. And when the young ones are big enough to eat solid food, all heck really starts to break loose for the mother cat. Not only does she then have to provide prey, but she also has to teach her young how to hunt (DRAWING).**

**When the nesting place doesn't seem secure enough for whatever reason, the mother cat will relocate her young without further ado. Like most wild animals, she almost always knows of a few alternative sites. The reflexive "limp response" of the young facilitates the difficult task of moving the family.**

**When the mother isn't in the nest with her young, the kittens remain very quiet. This is instinctive protective behavior that often allows them to escape detection by enemies. Most often they sleep at this time, nestled close to one another.**

# BIRTH AND RAISING

tom can therefore pose a serious threat to helpless young kittens. If an opportunity presents itself, for instance, when the mother is absent for a short while, such a tom may become a killer and will make short work of biting the little ones to death. Whatever we humans may think of this behavior, from the tom's point of view, the situation has been handled strategically and cleverly. He usually achieves his goal by means of this "cruel" strategy: After a few days the female gets over the loss of her young and she is soon calling for a tomcat again. If he then gets a move on, he can be the father of the next litter. Systematic "infanticide" just like that of newly arrived tomcat-despots has also been observed among lions and tigers.

**There are few young animals more charming than young kittens in their age of discovery. Their insatiable curiosity and untiring willingness to play pushes them to investigate or try out everything that comes their way.**

## From Infant Kitten to Teenager

At the third week the kittens become rapidly more mobile. They now undertake short excursions from their nest. At the age of four to five weeks their senses are mature and just as efficient as those of an adult. Motor development, however, takes a lot longer. This is no different with kittens than with human children. In walking, climbing, and leaping they lack not only agility, but also experience. At any rate, the kittens are now capable of retracting their claws and, if necessary, putting them out again. Up to this point their claws were continually extended.

Sheltered and cared for by their mother, the kittens quickly get bigger. They grow and grow, and consequently need more and more food. By the end of their first week their birth weight has already doubled; by the end of the first month it will have doubled again. Then, as soon as the little ones practice walking and climbing, the increase in weight slows down somewhat. Despite this, it is easy to see that, at some time, the mother won't be able to produce enough milk to satisfy all the kittens. This is when weaning begins. Just when the

kittens reach this stage depends on the size of the litter, as well as on the state of the mother's health and her dietary situation. Females put a lot of physical energy and reserves into milk production. Toward the end of the nursing period, they often look decidedly emaciated.

So, at four weeks, sometimes at six weeks or so, the kittens start consuming solid food as well. For cats living with a human family, the young simply accompany their mother to the food dish and sample what is offered there. Once these kittens are weaned, they can live independently of their mother. Free-ranging females bring prey from their hunting excursions back home to their young, and her kittens often stay with their mother longer to learn hunting techniques. Many females choose this time to settle their young in yet another nest. While the previous nest was selected on the criteria of safety and obscurity, the female now favors a spot from where she can easily hunt or reach other sources of food. Proximity now preempts safety.

The percentage of solid food in the overall diet of the kittens keeps increasing. Usu-

Week by week the kittens become more independent. Enthusiastically they try to imitate adult cats, as with these kittens cleaning themselves (ABOVE). Yet, for many of the necessary contortions their legs are still too short, their bellies too fat, their sense of balance too underdeveloped, and so they often tumble over in the process. Still, kittens don't give up that easily. In the end they will all know how to groom themselves as perfectly as their mother.

When the mother's milk is gradually no longer enough to satisfy the young ones, the time has come for them to try solid food (CENTER). No doubt about it, it tastes good!

Nevertheless, it's always nice when mother "lets herself be talked into it" and gives them one more milk meal (BELOW). After all, suckling doesn't just appease the hunger in the stomach, it also satisfies the need for security and warmth.

## At what age should kittens move to a new home?

You've found good homes among your circle of friends for your cat's kittens? And the future owners are already asking when they can pick up their kitten? Well, the answer is at the cat's hour: It's best not too soon and not too late.

Although with most kittens the transition from mother's milk to solid food is over by the eighth week, you could wait a little longer before separating the kittens from their mother. Though it is believed that a cat's socialization skills can be taught by humans, kittens at this age are still intensively learning. There are some things, such as hunting, that no human, no matter how well meaning, can teach them. On the other hand, the younger the kitten, the easier it is for it to adapt to a new home with new people and new living habits (assuming it is no longer dependent on its mother).

The best time to move a kitten into a new family, I believe, is around twelve weeks. It will probably call for its mother and littermates for a day or two, but then it will devote itself completely to scouting out its new surroundings. The mother cat, who so conscientiously looked after her children while they were still little, will not look long for her young at this point. She will already have gradually distanced herself from her litter during the weaning stage.

Climbing a tree trunk, now that's something worth learning. Going up isn't too bad, but going down . . . Ugh! Hard! At six weeks of age these littermates are doing their climbing exercises.

ally at eight weeks they are ready to live off solid food exclusively. This doesn't mean, however, that the source of milk instantly dries up. Often the kittens may nurse for a good while yet, if the mother will allow it. They continue to suckle partially to snack but mostly when they seek security.

At between the tenth and twelfth week of life, kittens begin to exhibit their true eye color. Up to this point all baby kittens have blue eyes because initially the iris is only sparsely pigmented. The definitive coloring of the iris is complete only in the second year of life.

At around four months the kittens' baby teeth start being replaced by permanent ones. The last baby tooth is replaced by a permanent tooth by the age of eight months, at the latest. There is generally no point looking for the kitten's lost baby teeth; they have very likely been swallowed.

Young farm cats or free-ranging street cats stay with their mother until they are six to eight months old. Then the little family group dissolves. By that time the feline teenagers have made numerous excursions and are acquainted with the territory in the general vicinity of their home. They have learned the ways and manners of cats and have been assimilated into the cat society there. In short, they have become independent feline personalities.

**So, they've all managed that and are sitting in the highest branch (ABOVE). They aren't worried yet about how to get down again.**

**Littermates at this age almost always stay close to one another in their exciting endeavors. As a group they can look any enemy (even if only imagined) in the eye: There is strength in numbers**

**This nine-week-old Chartreuse kitten (BELOW) has already developed an astonishing independence. Its reconnaissance paths lead it high over roofs. This isn't entirely without danger for this still-inexperienced kit-**

**ten. Falls happen at this age more often than you might think, and the "landing response" reflex that allows a falling cat to land on its feet develops only gradually.**

69

# PLAYING AND LEARNING

In their tireless play, little kittens not only learn to control their bodies, they also acquire all the other skills that help them thrive later in life as well. Cats also like to play when they are grown up, and as highly intelligent animals they can still learn new things quickly when they are older. They are by no means the untrainable loners they are often thought to be. A cat just doesn't always see why it should provide proof of its obedience at any particular time.

A kitten, when it comes into the world, is endowed with an entire set of innate behaviors. Instinctively it searches for the mother's teats, calls for help when it has wandered from the nest, or stays quiet as a mouse while the mother cat is briefly absent and the nest is vulnerable. When and why it has to behave this way are not things it has to learn first. It simply "knows." Its instincts, which it inherited from its forebears living in the wild, tell it what has to be done. But this innate knowledge does not suffice to get the cat through its entire life. There is still a lot to learn.

## All Beginnings Are Hard

There are two kinds of learning: learning useful behavior and appropriate responses through interaction with the environment, and learning patterns of movement through exercise and training. Little kittens are avid and gifted subjects in both kinds of learning. The stronger their muscles get, the more lively the kittens in the nest become. After three weeks, they make their first attempts to leave the nest. It isn't all that easy to keep all four legs under control and not go tumbling about, but thanks to the persistence of the young in practicing, by the age of six to seven weeks the kittens can move around, run, and jump like adult cats. By this age they have already rehearsed more difficult types of movement, such as balancing on a chair or even on a narrow slat. It is not until they are three months old, though, that their ability

# CAT CHILDREN

Kittens find anything that wobbles, dangles, walks, rolls, or moves any old way and has a handy size irresistibly attractive. Christmas tree baubles, hollow Easter eggs, or streamers are just as much fun to play with as small branches, dry leaves, or Mother's tail.

# PLAYING AND LEARNING

**Playfully, the kittens exercise the various skills they will need in life: getting hold of something in a trice (LEFT), patiently lying in wait (RIGHT), and, of course, fighting feline style. Already at the tender age of three weeks, they are scrapping with their littermates in the nest (FAR RIGHT). In contrast to the voluble play of puppies, kittens at play hardly ever utter a sound, only letting out a shriek when their playmate has, for example, grabbed them too roughly.**

to coordinate leg movements and to totally maintain their balance is fully matured.

In the very first weeks of life the kittens start to lick their own fur. At first this procedure looks touchingly awkward, but soon it goes quite smoothly—at least for those easy-to-reach parts of the body. By the age of six or seven weeks, the kittens have mastered the art of washing their faces with their front paws

in that inimitable feline manner. As soon as the little ones begin wandering from the nest and consuming food in addition to the mother's milk, they learn to take care of their "business" feline fashion. In general, at five to six weeks the kittens can keep their eliminations under control. But where will these treasures be deposited when nature sounds its call? On their reconnaissance

tours with their mother the kittens learn the location of the litter box or a suitable place in the open country to distribute

**Strong, healthy kittens enjoy movement—just as human children do. This little four-week-old fellow is bouncing around like a rubber ball.**

their offerings, where they instinctively scratch in the loose soil or sand to cover their feces.

## Learning While Playing

From the fourth week, kittens begin to play, beginning, among others, with "social games." First they timidly bat at their littermates and their mother with their paws, but soon they begin to practice swatting and biting more purposefully. Once they are surer on their feet, the games become more distinctive and lively. Soon they are frolicking and gamboling in merry chases over the open ground, careening like rubber balls in wild flight over the ever-expanding play area.

Later, around the age of seven weeks, the frequency of social games decreases and "object-related" games assume increasing significance. Small objects that either move by themselves, or can be propelled by the cats' paws, become cat toys, whether they were intended to be or not. If suitable objects are not to be found, many kittens engage in freewheeling games (or ludic activity) with objects that exist only in their imagination! They jump up at walls to catch imaginary flies or chase invisible objects across the floor, all the while vigorously batting the objects with their paws. Of course, the kittens' own tails, or that of their mother, are fine toys and, moreover, they are always at hand.

## Caution: Danger of accidents for inexperienced kittens!

If you have young kittens in your house, you should make potential trouble spots as safe as you can. Take a moment to look at the surroundings of the nest and house from the perspective of a kitten and think where you, as a clumsy baby kitten, might fall down, or later, as a curious young kitten, might run into trouble. Examples of accidents waiting to happen are stairs with open steps or open railings, and balustrades and balconies, especially when a smooth floor covering offers no grip to the kittens' claws. Unfortunately, young kittens have been known to sustain internal injuries in unlucky falls. It is not until it is four to five weeks old that a kitten can turn its body during freefall to land on its feet (and even then, a relatively long fall might hurt an older kitten or cat).

Later on, when the kittens are exploring, the same sources of danger exist for them as for small children: hot plates that are turned on, any kind of poison or chemical left standing around open, electric wires, and so forth. Try, if possible, to prevent accidents, but be aware in so doing that you can't tie the little ones up.

## Use and Purpose of Playing

As to why young animals play, the usual answer is that it is a method of developing the necessary physical skills and agility to be able to strike out successfully in later life. That is doubtless an important aspect of playing, but it is far from its only purpose.

A kitten that plays with various objects (or prey, as well) learns their characteristics. A dry leaf, for example, is much easier to throw up into the air than a piece of wood, while if you try to do the same thing with a stone of similar size, all you get is sore paws. A little branch will not walk away if you take your eyes off it for a moment; a beetle, on the other hand, will disappear into the

grass. With a mouse, you could easily get bitten on the nose. Like any child, the kitten has a lot to learn before it knows its way around the things in its world, and a good part of that it learns through its tireless play.

In play with others of their kind or with playmates of another species, the main thing kittens learn is how others react to their actions. This is how they learn appropriate social behavior. Cats that have to grow up without playmates of their own kind often become social outcasts, whereas cats that play extensively with peo-

ple when they are young get to know and understand people almost as well as they know their own kind. These cats usually make particularly friendly housemates. The same holds true of cats that grow up in the company of dogs or other animals.

The main biological purpose of play is physical training, because through play an animal can gain a great deal of experience without danger to life and limb. Playing is seen only among highly developed animals, such as mammals and some birds. It has been asserted that the most intelligent among these groups of animals are those that enjoy a long and sheltered childhood,

**How does my mother do that so well? She makes it look so easy when she climbs up a tree. Well, there must be some way to do it, it would be ridiculous otherwise. I just can't give up . . .**

when they have particularly rich opportunities for play. Without a doubt, after primates and whales, playful predators, including cats, are among the most intelligent of animals.

## The Mother as Educator

A mother cat is endowed with a large dose of patience. She needs it, too, because she continually serves as a piece of gymnastic equipment or as an object of practice for various battle tactics—in short, as an understanding playmate. Only when the mother thinks the kittens have become too ram-

bunctious will she rebuke them with a short hiss or a slap to the face.

The mother cat is also an important model for the kittens. Curious and eager to learn as they now are, they learn a lot from watching adult cats and imitating them.

As soon as the young are ready to function outside the nest, the mother leads them out: the female in the lead and the little ones, with their tails straight up in the air, in single file behind. This becomes part of the new routine. You are left with the impression that the mother wants to show her young everything that is important on these ever-lengthening walks. Now and then,

she shoos the flock of kittens back into a protective cluster with hisses and paw swipes when she is frightened by something or when she spots danger—real or imagined—perhaps in the shape of a lawnmower or the neighbor's dog. By such protective behavior, the mother imparts an image of enemies or threatening situations to the minds of the young. Mind you, cats are able, later as adults, to modify these learned images through new experiences. A kitten taught to be afraid of dogs is quite capable of learning to be friendly with dogs in later life.

**Did it! Finally got up in the tree! A successful climb like this one strengthens the self-confidence of the six-week-old kitten enormously. Except—how do you get down again? Young kittens regularly overestimate their capability and often get themselves into precarious situations. Immediately a plaintive mewing for its mother resounds. She will probably just lick the little one a bit, soothingly, and finally croon to coax it until it manages the way down on its own. Our brave little kitten here dares to leap to solid ground even without the intervention of its mother.**

In playful skirmishes, kittens learn to correctly interpret the gestures and expressions of their cat companions. Anybody ignoring an anxious-annoyed defensive posture such as the one taken by this crouching kitten (ABOVE LEFT) risks getting a proper swat in the face (ABOVE RIGHT).

Fighting games (BELOW LEFT) differ from real fights in that they proceed "restrictedly," the individual roles can change repeatedly and rapidly, besides which the adversaries are very easy to distract. A serious fighter could not permit himself to pause or glance away (BELOW RIGHT); his opponent would immediately take advantage of such a lapse.

## A Lesson in Hunting Skills

When the kittens are about four weeks old, the mother begins teaching hunting skills. To do this, she brings home mice or other prey she has killed. The little ones are allowed to play with the booty and sniff it for a short while. At this stage, the mother most often eats the prey by herself. At most, the youngsters might take an occasional nibble, chewing on it

**To develop social behavior typical of cats, it is extremely important for the kitten to practice appropriate role behavior in play. To impress, threaten, attack, submit, and also, in all fairness, to let the underdog opponent prevail, are all easiest to learn when playing with littermates.**

for a while before finally swallowing it. They don't do this because they are hungry (after all, they are still nursing) but rather out of curiosity and because they are imitating their mother's example.

About two weeks later, the mother brings home the first live mouse. Cooing, she utters a very special "mouse" call, at which the kittens immediately come running. There follows a detailed demonstration of how

to handle a mouse and how to react when it runs away or defends itself. The mother lets the mouse go, catches it again, pounces on it, pins it down, and generally "plays" with the mouse. It is a lesson with authentic visual aids. As you can easily imagine, the mouse cannot last long at this game. As

it begins to tire, the young venture into the fray, the pluckier ones in the lead. With the mother supplying watchful supervision and ready to prevent the escape of the mouse, the kittens extend tentative paws toward the mouse and jump back in surprise when the mouse attacks with aggressive

**For an older cat in need of rest, a teenage feline with its continual demands to play can become a real pest.**

squeaks. Gradually the feline pupils become more self-assured and attempt to make grabs for the mouse. They are promptly made aware of the sharp teeth of their intended victim. Ouch! The mouse is dropped and makes its escape. The kittens have been warned and have learned that prey are not toys but opponents able to put up a fight, and that they are to be taken seriously. From now on, caution becomes second nature to the kittens.

So the mother brings home mouse after mouse to practice on. It requires many hours of study before the kittens develop the necessary skills to catch prey expertly and confidently. Actually, the kittens don't have to be taught the movements essential to catching prey: lying in wait, stalking, grabbing with the paws, and pouncing. These are innate behaviors that have been practiced many times

## Mice and birds deposited by the door—does it have to be this way?

You want to have a young cat but have a hard time coming to terms with the fact that this means you will be bringing a predator into your house? Then you should pay attention when selecting a kitten and either choose one that has grown up in a home where there was no possibility of going out or one whose mother is not a hunter. For the hunting experiences a young cat has in its first sixteen to twenty weeks of life largely dictate whether it will become a predator or not, and the kind of prey it will favor.

There is no guarantee that the offspring will turn out just like their mother. I can only repeat that cats are definitely individuals.

Some of them are completely self-sufficient when it comes to learning and teach themselves, even in advanced age, what others were taught by their mothers when they were young. So, if you absolutely don't want to find a dead mouse on your carpet or risk threatening your neighbor's bluebird houses, you really should reconsider whether a cat would be a suitable pet for you. Or, consider the advantages of keeping an indoor cat.

Conversely, it also holds true that if you want a cat to decimate a mouse population, you should try to pick out a young cat you know has been well trained by its mother in the art of catching mice.

during play. What they do have to learn, however, is to assess the reactions of the prey and to respond accordingly. Another activity that must be learned is how to apply the killing bite after the prey has been caught. To develop this skill, the kitten must first overcome a natural inhibition about biting. This inhibition is important to prevent kittens from biting their littermates, although kittens do learn to simulate biting the sides of the other kittens' necks during play. Ultimately, however, in the heat of the battle with the prey, the kitten sheds this natural inhibition and delivers a killing bite to the prey. This is a turning point in the animal's development—from now on the cat is a hunter of mice (see the chapter "The Hunter and the Hunted").

Partially through experience and also through lessons from their mother, the kittens learn what varieties of prey, besides mice, are available and what kinds should be avoided. Bees that buzz over the lawn and are ready targets for a paw can inflict painful stings. Shrews taste awful. Rats, it's true, can provide a substantial meal, but they are truly dangerous adversaries. Even when the mother is an experienced rat hunter, she will not bring the kittens a live rat until they are already experienced hunters because of the danger of being seriously wounded by the wildly attacking rodent. Scientific studies on the development of predatory behavior in cats have shown that mother cats are excessively cautious when exposing their young to rats. Even when kittens had previously demonstrated success in dealing with rats, if the mother was present, she would not allow the kittens to hunt the rat. She would always step in to finish the dangerous task herself.

**Just as well that the mother is always around during those early outings, checking to see whether danger is lurking nearby.**

## The Games Adult Cats Play

The maturing of the kitten does not signal an end to its play life. It is true that playful behavior decreases in frequency, but most cats continue to play throughout their lives. Just like people, some become painfully serious, while others retain their youthful playfulness. How often an adult cat plays does not only depend on its temperament, it mainly depends on its environment. Playing helps to fill the time that is not used for activities essential to survival. We know that animals in zoos spend much more time at play than comparable animals in the wild. Wild animals need to expend considerable effort and strength obtaining food, defending their territories, migrating as the seasons demand, and protecting themselves from natural enemies. Well-tended, sheltered house cats find themselves in totally different circumstances. They can afford to engage in a little game at almost any time, and often they actually need to do so. Playing affords them an opportunity to employ innate instincts and responses not readily used in their sedentary existence. The typical game, then, consists of instinctive actions or traces of those actions. It differs from the serious use of these innate traits only in that these traits

When the young are big enough to leave the protection of the nest for a while, the mother cat takes them on short excursions into the countryside. The female leads and her young follow, tails high in the air, in single file (ABOVE).

When the mother has caught prey, the youngsters can hardly contain themselves. Yet they also occasionally have to watch how she handles the mouse herself (CENTER).

The youngsters don't like having a refreshing nap very much. They look for a way to pass the time. So, mother will just have to become a piece of playground equipment, whether she wants to or not (BELOW).

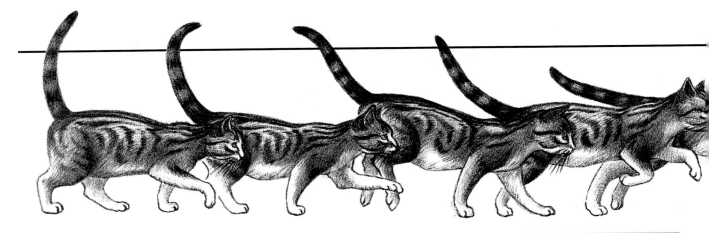

Cats sleep a lot, it's true, but when they are awake they have an enormous urge to move and occupy themselves. In the indoor environment, where they don't have to hunt to survive, they simply play. There are running games, when the cat sprints off from a standing position as if it were running for its life (drawing); agility games, for instance, when a dangling cord is supposed to be caught; fighting games, when the rug or bedspread takes over the role of adversary; and finally, action motivated purely by curiosity, for example, when open drawers are investigated.

and actions can change rapidly and are often repeated countless times without any specific goal being achieved.

Many cats like to play catch with one another as well as with human playmates. In these games the cat scuttles, threatens, escapes, pursues, and tussles. For any participant, even a human one, it is easily recognizable as a frivolous activity. The claws remain in and the bites are merely threatened. Another favorite game is "hand-to-hand combat," with the cat employing its hind legs.

It is similar to a form of tomcat fighting where one of the rivals lies on the ground, clasps the other with its forelegs, and simultaneously, with kicking hind legs, works over the opponent's stomach. In the house, a sofa cushion, sweater, or teddy bear may well assume the role of the adversary. To a large extent, the play activities of adult cats are vestigial remnants of the behaviors used in hunting and vanquishing prey (see the chapter "The Hunter and Hunted"). Totally housebound cats, in particular, often play hunting games for want of any real possibilities to hunt, with persistence and enthusi-

**A ball of yarn, such an age-old and eternal kitten's toy, is always appropriate and is loved by old and young cats alike.**

## Indoor cat games

Put in a regular "game hour" with your cat. This doesn't just keep the cat young and fit, it will also be beneficial and relaxing for you, you'll see. Besides, even the liveliest cat will get tired sometime during the game. So, through a controlled game program, the cat can be kept away from games it thinks up by itself that might have a destructive effect on the furniture. Indoor cats, especially, like to have some small object be an interesting prey animal in their fantasy and will sneak up on it with their tail twitching in excitement. Unfortunately, some knick-knacks may not weather the storm undamaged, even though the final pounce on the prey is inevitably executed with re-

markable precision. The cat just needs an outlet to work out its pent-up hunting instinct. Give it one! This needn't be an expensive furry, squeaky toy mouse from some chic boutique selling cat accessories. A spool, the famous ball of yarn, or a tennis ball will do the trick. One of my cat's favorite games is to "work over" a crumpled-up, loose sheet of paper. After he has fought it at length with thrusts of his hind legs, he conscientiously shreds it up with his paws and teeth. He considers his task accomplished when bits of paper are spread all over the rug like confetti. So, every time as I go to get the piece of paper, I go to get the vacuum cleaner out as well.

**A cat that associates unpleasant memories, such as a trip to see the veterinarian, with carriers will, from then on, do everything in its power to resist being stuck inside the container again.**

asm—mostly to the great amusement of their owners. They will fly after a rubber ball here, fish around to get a ball of yarn out from under the closet there, and toss toy mice up in the air like circus jugglers to catch them again in their paws in almost the same instant. These are merely elements of natural cat motions involved in catching prey. On closer examination, there are three distinct catching techniques for the various prey: first, for catching mice (pouncing, pinning down, biting to death); second, for snagging birds (leaping high into the air, swiping to bring down prey with the forepaws); third, surprise angling to catch fish. Outside at the pond, the cat dips its paw into the water in a twinkling and flips the fish over its shoulder onto dry land. Then it quickly turns and pounces on it as it would on normal land-based prey. Even if very few cat owners have been able to observe their cats catching fish out in nature, most know the relevant behavior of their lounge leopard from play hour at home.

Incidentally, quite a few cats have mastered the art of retrieving just as well as dogs (except rarely on command and always just when they want to play), and they drag their toys over so that people can toss or roll them. Another game that most cats get excited about is the one involving crinkly tissue paper or wrapping paper. Some cats will hide underneath it; others want someone to rustle it around so they can lie in wait before pouncing on it.

## Cat Intelligence

Scientifically speaking, intelligence, learning, and memory are phenomena that are still riddled with mystery. Despite intensive worldwide research, we still don't know what, for instance, happens in the nervous system during the process of learning, or in which portion of the brain memory is located. There is no doubt, however, that intelligence and the ability to learn play a large role, at least in the lives of all the more highly developed mammals. Among these animals, natural elements of behavior contain, as a rule, only short sequences of movement that are then, through learning, serialized in various ways and practically applied in given situations. We shouldn't simply equate the concept of "intelligence" in animals with our own "cleverness." Animals can't solve mathematical equations or set up theoretical thought constructs. Rather, they have what is termed "practical intelligence," which means they can understand contexts, store experiences in memory, and find feasible solutions for getting around obstacles, extricating themselves from tight

**Some cats go so far as to learn that in the world of people, even natural prey, such as mice, are taboo (ABOVE LEFT).**

**Cats close to families quickly understand that little four-legged creatures are also to be considered family members—and as such should not be eaten (ABOVE RIGHT).**

**A cat quickly learns to prepare itself for certain regular events. For instance, in the morning it will sit punctually at the stroke of seven in front of the door and wait to be let in (BELOW LEFT).**

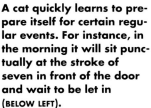

**This farm cat learned long ago when milking time rolls around and sits by the stall door in anticipation of its ration of milk (BELOW RIGHT).**

## What's the best way to train a cat?

It's easiest when the cat is still young. What Tiger didn't learn, Tiger will still learn without any trouble, but usually not as quickly or as easily. The important things are delineating clearly between what is and what is not permitted, and instituting hard-and-fast consequences for breaking the rules once they're established. Someone who for months forbids the cat to jump up on the dinner table and one day, out of politeness, allows rash guests to feed it from their plates can instantly throw out the window all the preceding educational achievements. And, to misquote another proverb: Trust is fine, but control is the only thing that's reliable with cats! When the cream pie is already on the coffee table while you're still out in the hall chatting with your guests and all the doors are open—well, sure, you asked for it.

As a tried-and-true educational tool for cats, the raised human voice that says a clear "No," a firm hand-clap, as well as more drastic measures like a squirt gun, have all paid off. They quickly make it clear to a cat that it should stop what it's doing right away—provided the punishing action follows immediately, which means while the cat is still engaged in its unwelcome action. The jet from a squirt gun has the advantage of working over some distance, so the cat connects the sudden dreadful downpour with, say, the forbidden flower pot in which it was just digging, instead of associating the punishment with you. Don't punish your cat by striking out at it, not even with a rolled-up newspaper or similar weapon. In the long run, you will make the cat scared of hand movements.

You will reinforce desirable behavior best with a lot of praise and much stroking, or even with a couple of nuggets to nibble on. The latter you should strictly ration, out of consideration for the cat's physique.

spots, or reaching the things they wish to reach. In other words, the intelligence of animals enables them to survive under the most variable conditions. In nature, a "slow-witted" animal has as little chance of surviving as a blind or lame one.

As a predator whose prey is not only stalwart but wary as well, the cat needs a goodly amount of tactical intelligence. It has an outstanding ability to learn, not only as a young animal but still as an adult. Cats learn not only according to the principle of trial and error, like many other animals, but also simply by watching. If a cat has the opportunity, for instance, to observe a companion jumping up and opening door latches, it will learn the same trick (usually to the dismay of its owner) much more quickly than if it had had to gain the knowledge on its own.

**Whoever enjoys training can easily teach a cat a few little tricks, such as sitting up. Cats quickly understand what their human friends expect of them.**

## Training and Obedience

There is a widespread rumor that cats can't be trained. Why should cats, with their notable ability to learn, not understand how they should behave amongst people? As little kittens they certainly caught on when their mother taught them feline etiquette and the ground rules for getting along with other cats. All we have to do is to communicate to the family cat, in a clear and consistent manner, the rules that now apply in living with a human family. An ill-mannered cat is really only a reflection of the pedagogical incompetence of its owner—or of the owner's exaggerated or unrealistic expectations.

Cats learn easily what is permitted and what isn't, except they don't always see why it is they should follow those rules. In the presence of a person, this "super cat" that dominates the territory indoors, it makes sense to follow this person's wishes and not go swing on the drapes or traipse around on the table. Most cats prefer to avoid conflict, but when this person just happens not to be around . . .

**Cat training must be well thought out. Excessive responses can scare cats so badly that they are simply frightened instead of being cured of bad habits. Just about every cat will become an occasional thief when the aroma of the Sunday roast fills the air. Sliced onion, garlic, or lemon held in front of its nose will put it off even the tastiest roast.**

**To shoo a cat away from a spot, a sharp clap of the hands or a "No!" will suffice.**

**Especially effective educational tools once again turn out to be squirt guns, sprayers, or atomizers.**

**Still, one thing applies to all punishment: It must be forthcoming during the wrong-doing, not after the fact. Otherwise the cat can't see the connection.**

# THE HUNTER AND THE HUNTED

Of all predators, the cat is the perfect hunter. With keen senses, an unbelievably lithe body, and reactions of lightning speed, it pursues its prey. A cat, especially one that seldom has the opportunity to hunt, often plays with its prey for a long time before it kills it with a decisive bite to the neck. In this way, it gives vent to its bottled-up hunting instinct.

**C**ats catch mice, lots of mice! After all, that was the original reason they lived with people. While it is true that by selective breeding people have created a wide variety of breeds and colors, all these centuries the cat's natural behavior has remained largely unchanged. Cats are and will remain predators. People should always be aware of this when sharing their homes with such nimble and light-footed hunters.

### The Hunting Instinct

The hunting instinct is natural to cats. As little kittens they discover and practice the necessary elements of movement for hunting without outside instruction. Throughout its life a cat is forced by an innate drive to apply these sequences of movement—whether or not a suitable occasion for such movement presents itself.

Particular perceptions release an overriding urge to chase and to catch. A trigger for such movement—also called an unconditioned, or key, stimulus—is often the rapid passage of a small object on the ground within reach of the cat. It could be it a paper ball or a mouse; the cat just has to leap after it. If a long period of time passes without a suitable trigger, the cat will start to look for a substitute. The object no longer has to be as big as a mouse, a fly will do; instead of pouncing on a moving object on the ground, it could pounce on a clock pendulum or baubles hanging from a Christmas tree. A cat that hasn't lived out its hunting urge for a long time can be seen catching imaginary birds or mice made of air. Such play, or ludic activity, serves in some measure to release the pent-up hunting urge.

The hunting instinct has nothing to do with how full a cat is either. When a house cat pounces on its toy mouse, it does not mean it is hungry and must be fed at once. By generously feeding your cat, you cannot prevent it hunting "real" prey as soon as it gets the opportunity. Conversely, farmers do not gain anything by not feeding their cats in the hopes they will catch a lot of mice. Well-fed cats don't roam as far in search of prey as starving strays, but catch their mice in the vicinity of the house and barn—no more or less than they would catch on an empty stomach.

**It requires not only an excellent mastery of the body, but also quite a bit of experience to catch such a nimble rodent. Young cats start honing their skills on "practice" mice their mother brings back for them from her hunting expeditions.**

**Obstacles such as this little brook are no problem for a cat on the hunt. In a single elegant leap, it simply vaults over it. With their enormously powerful hind legs, cats are able to jump up to four feet (1.2 meters) wide and six and one-half feet (two meters) high from a standing position.**

**The litheness and baffling physical control that cats have become particularly evident when one day they actually do fall down from somewhere. They almost always land on all fours. The tail serves as a rudder to turn the body the right way up, and the arching of the back during the last phase of the fall lessens the impact.**

## Hunting Time

The wild ancestors of our house cats were active predominately in the half-light of twilight and in the dark, just as their wild relatives are today. For the domestic cat this no longer applies to the same extent; it is on its feet—and on the hunt—during the day as well. About 50 percent of its prey is caught in broad daylight, some 20 percent during the hours around dawn and dusk, and a mere 30 percent at night. In the summertime, though, cats avoid the hot daylight hours for such a strenuous activity as hunting, and do indeed go out in the cooler night. In the win-

tertime it is the other way around. Then most cats hunt during the afternoon, when it is warmest.

It is striking that many cats go off stalking when it is drizzling slightly or immediately after a cloudburst. (Their proverbial fear of water doesn't count for much!) We don't know what it is that drives the cat into the drenched fields. Possibly, prey is less observant then.

## Physical Requirements

The main requirements for a hunter are keen senses, to track down prey, and a good control of the body, to be able to pursue and overpower prey. The cat has plenty of both. The ability of a cat to land on all fours every time it falls is proverbial. It races with incredible power, bounding from the ground, climbs trees vertically like a person wearing crampons (except much faster), balances with elegant confidence on narrow beams or branches, and executes the farthest leap with baffling, unerring accuracy. Its eyes, aligned to the front and focused straight ahead, enable good depth perception, a prerequisite for a precise gauging of distances. The ability, unique in the animal realm, to

A cat can squeeze itself through incredibly narrow slits. Whatever the head will fit through, the rest of the body can cram itself through too.

be able to retract and extend its claws gives the cat further invaluable advantages for hunting. (More about these anatomical particularities can be found in the chapter "Origin and Species.")

Yet, in spite of perfect equipment, hunting is an arduous business. Only about one in four attempts ends in success. And mice, the natural main food for a cat, are just small snacks for the hunter. It would need to eat about twelve of them each day should it not get anything else.

## The Course of the Hunt

It all begins when the cat picks up a sound that makes it prick up its ears: a rustling in the leaves; the pitter-patter of mice feet; or a high, whispering squeak. The maneuverable ears of the cat turn this way and that. It attempts to determine the direction from which the promising sound is coming, and then the cat stares spellbound in that direction.

### Creeping Up and Jumping Accurately

If the cat has discovered that its prey is some distance away, it will walk toward it low to the ground, but relatively quickly, utilizing any piece of cover around. Some yards closer, it stops suddenly and assumes a typical lying-in-wait stance: belly close to the ground, legs markedly crooked beneath the body, head extended far to the

**Cats do not have collar bones, the bone that in other animals connects the shoulder blades to the thorax. This means a cat can move its forelegs freely out to the sides. For climbing, this is an invaluable asset, as the cat can literally "embrace" the tree trunk.**

# THE HUNTER AND THE HUNTED

**Sneaking up . . . crouching down . . . a quick pounce—and there, it's got a mouse! Only don't let it get away!**

front, and ears noticeably aimed forward. Thus it remains, motionless. Only the tip of its tail twitches occasionally and betrays the extreme tension of the moment. For minutes at a time, the cat can observe its prey from this position. If the distance still appears too great for an attack, the cat begins a second "creep," or sneaks closer extremely slowly and carefully, step by step. In suitable cover, it then takes up the lying-in-wait stance once

again. Finally, it prepares itself for the take-off, slowly maneuvering its hind legs farther forward and suggesting light rhythmic treading movements with its back feet. The cat resembles a track-and-field athlete who takes delicate little steps shortly before the running start for the long jump.

Then the cat darts forward unexpectedly. Rarely (for instance, in tall grass) does it pounce on its victim in a single, powerful bound. Most often it dashes toward it. A cat experienced at hunting undertakes the final leap so close to the prey that it can reach and grab it with its forepaws without its back feet leaving the ground.

This means it can still correct its course during the pounce or lengthen the leap to follow the evasive tactics of its prey. The cat spreads its hind legs wide apart to brace itself and slow down its momentum. This stance gives the cat the necessary stability for a possible fight with the prey and at the same time offers the option of doubling back on the spot should the prey prove to be too adversarial.

A cat that has been lying in wait on a branch or on top of a wall may attack from this elevated position. If it does so, however, it never jumps directly from the height down onto its victim but drops to the ground right next to it. From there it pounces on its prey in the way just described.

Should the prey escape because it noticed its attacker just in time, or because the cat's leap missed the mark, most cats won't give up right away. They pursue their victims at a run and sometimes catch them anyway.

## Fighting with Prey

A cat can dispatch a captured grasshopper or butterfly without any effort, but a mouse that's fighting for its life in the clutches of a cat is an adversary to be taken very seriously. To put it bluntly: The mouse stands a fair chance. When their lives are on the line, mice become truly fearless fighters. If the cat doesn't hold them by the neck in a tight grip right from the start, a good many mice actually start nipping at

**The cat has spied a tiny movement in the grass. It remains motionless, belly to the ground and head extended far to the front, lying in wait for a chance to pounce on its prey.**

the cat. The latter, startled, backs off—and as soon as it does so the mouse takes to its heels. If it's lucky, its head start is enough to let it get away. Rats, being larger, make for profitable prey, but they are much more aggressive and put up a heftier fight than mice. A house cat certainly needs a healthy dose of courage and experience in hunting to seriously challenge a fully grown brown rat. Most inexperienced cats that attack a rat like this are beaten by its vehement counterattacks during its escape, but there are also heroic cats that are able to overpower rats in a drawn-out battle.

To overpower a rat, the cat usually doesn't get involved in

**A cat does not wander aimlessly through its hunting grounds in search of prey. If it has had success in a certain place once, it will keep coming back to that spot for days. Its motto is: Where there's one mouse, there's more. A cat will wait in front of a mouse hole with infinite patience. Should the unsuspecting mouse finally make an appearance, the game's up for the mouse. The cat's long whiskers virtually enfold the captured mouse and help the cat keep track of its squirming prisoner.**

**Cats enjoy playing with their prey for a while before eating it, in many cases even before they have killed it. With anxious cats still inexperienced at hunting, this game—which appears so cruel to us—may help the cat assess how dangerous the prey is and how it reacts. On the other hand, cats that seldom have the opportunity to hunt use this windfall to vent their pent-up hunting urges. They put off the well-aimed fatal bite in the prey's neck because they simply can't bring themselves to end the hunt right away. They have to be very careful, though, that in all their playing around, the mouse doesn't manage to get away.**

a tussling match. Rather, it draws back a bit after the first pounce, gathers itself for a renewed attempt, and attacks again a dozen times or more until the rat's resistance finally weakens. The cat's repeated attacks are so quick that it is difficult to see what happens in detail. In the end, however, the rat lies on the ground, done for—and the cat often has a few deep wounds in its skin.

With a few larger prey, the cat often doesn't let go again once it has clamped its teeth in the animal's neck. If the victim begins to writhe and struggle, the cat throws itself on its side, while holding its prey firmly between the claws of its forepaws, and works it over with powerful thrusts of its hind legs. (This fighting tactic can often be observed with wrestling kittens and adult cats still like to "fight" the hand of a human playmate this way, too.)

### The Fatal Bite in the Neck

In the end, whether directly after the first successful pounce or only after a longer struggle, the cat kills its prey. It does this in a way innate to all species of cats: with a bite to the neck. Its knifelike canine teeth, or fangs, are the perfect tools for this. Mind you, these pointed teeth are not suitable for biting down on something hard. (If this inadvertently happens to a cat, its canines can splinter pretty easily or break off completely.) These daggers can certainly penetrate the thin skull of a mouse, but they cannot crush its spine. Instead, in the fatal bite, the canine forces itself like a wedge between the cervical vertebrae and breaks them apart. The medulla is torn open—and the animal is dead on the spot.

To place the bite accurately, while biting, the cat makes a

series of rapid jaw movements that make it look like it's chattering its teeth—a kind of double-quick groping for a suitable spot. At the roots of the canines there are multiple sensory cells that react to pressure. Should the tip of the tooth bump on a hard bone, the cat loosens the grip of its jaws a little to allow the tooth to test a fractionally different spot. It repeats this until the tooth finally penetrates the gap between the two vertebrae.

Incidentally, a cat can sometimes be observed—while sitting on the windowsill, for example—watching birds outside. It suddenly starts to "chatter" with the corners of its mouth pulled back, and, indeed, its teeth actually are chattering. This is nothing but the killing bite just mentioned, which the cat is executing as if it already had one of the birds in its mouth. Behaviorists call

**Even when the cat isn't at all hungry, as a born hunter, it has to respond to its hunting instinct and "finish off" the mouse.**

something like this a ludic action. The stimulus of the birds—eagerly watched but out of reach—is so strong that the instinctive action of biting down is spontaneously generated in the cat.

## After a Successful Hunt

A cat must be close to collapsing from hunger if it starts eating its killed prey right away. Usually it just turns away "when the deed is done." It appears to suddenly lose all interest in its prey. It simply leaves it lying there, moves off a ways, and maybe sniffs at the ground or just starts cleaning itself. The purpose of all this is to relieve the tension of the preceding hunt and to give the cat time to calm down again. After a stroll like that, it will return to its prey and carry it around. Laying it down, sauntering off again, then picking up its prey can be repeated several times until the excited hunter has regained its peace of mind. Finally, the cat will usually carry (or drag, according to the size) its capture to a place that offers good shelter. There it will deservedly stuff itself.

In the eyes of cats, birds up to the size of pigeons are and always will be potential prey. Cats quickly understand, though, that caged birds are off-limits and accept the bird cage simply as a part of the room or patio decor.

A fat grasshopper may be easy to catch, but it is not very satisfying. Still, a cat can hardly let some hopping green thing hop on by untouched. And most cats eat such fat insects right away.

## What to do with what the cat drags in?

If they are allowed to go outside, even the loveliest lap cat or the most phlegmatic sofa tom will, sooner or later, arrive with a bloody, chewed-up animal in its mouth. Cats happen to be predators!

Therefore, be prepared for the occasion when your house companion lays a dead mouse at your feet by way of a present, or even worse, rollicks through the house with a victim that is literally bright-eyed and bushy-tailed. Even when the cat has no way of going outside, you cannot be assured that you will be spared such surprises. There are always careless birds that fly up to the window or onto the balcony right in front of the cat's nose.

Under no circumstances should you punish your cat, eager to hunt, for doing something so basic to its nature! The best thing is for you to quietly take the animal away at an opportune moment—as soon as the cat allows you to. That will be the best thing for your house and, under the circumstances, the best thing for your cat, too. And then, especially in urban areas these days, you have to reckon that mice will have some amount of chemical pesticides in them (and possibly because of this will have been half-dead and easy prey for the cat). The cat won't die from ingesting these pesticides, but such substances aren't exactly good for it either. Besides leaving traces of blood, birds that get worked over in the house by a cat often leave amazing amounts of feathers that are neither appetizing to look at nor easy to get rid of. Just one more reason why it's a good idea to remove that dead animal at the earliest opportunity.

From time to time, for no apparent reason, a cat completely loses interest in its prey, even before it has killed it. If the animal has been badly maimed in the classic cat-and-mouse game, you sometimes have no choice but to take on the sorry task of putting the victim out of its misery.

## "Cruelly" Toying with Prey

Some cats keep playing with the dead animal for some time before eating it. They swat at it with their paws and make the craziest leaps. The wilder and more persistent these leaps, the more difficult the victim was to overpower. The "dance" over prey (called overflow play) is a particularly effective way of getting rid of the tension of the hunt. The cat is, so to speak, venting its relief.

This kind of reaction is certainly understandable—it seems somehow human to us, after all—but why do so many cats play with their prey before they kill it? There are several reasons for this. First, an anxious cat, or one still inexperienced in hunting, plays with live prey to ascertain how dangerous it is and how it reacts, while overcoming its own fear. Second, the cat-and-mouse game intensifies the ex-

citement, helping the cat overcome its inborn inhibition against biting, and actually triggers the death bite. (For example, a mother cat uses a bite in the neck similar in technique and approach when transporting her young, only without the excitement of the hunt, which severely inhibits the bite.)

The third reason applies especially to cats that play because they rarely have the opportunity to catch prey and are therefore greedy for hunting activities. For a cat kept in an environment practically devoid of prey (such as an apartment cat that only has limited room to run outside or is restricted to a balcony), it must be a great event when it has actually caught a mouse or even a small bird. It can't bring itself to then put a cut-and-dried end to the hunt with a killing bite,

so it procrastinates as long as possible. In playing out each action of the hunt again and again, it is venting its hunting urge.

Another aspect comes into play when a mother cat brings her young a live animal to offer them instruction through demonstration and later the opportunity to practice (see the chapter "Playing and Learning").

## The Natural Array of Prey

In principle, a cat can carry off any animal that isn't bigger than it is; in practice, it rarely lays its paws on an animal larger than a rat or a pigeon.

The vast majority of cats are outstanding mousers—providing they are allowed to hunt.

This is the conclusion from a number of different investigations, ranging from those based on observed behavior to analyses of the stomach contents of cats that were shot or otherwise killed accidentally. Whether feral, free-ranging house, or farm cats, the results are the same: 70 to 90 percent of their diet consists of mice. The rest consists of kitchen scraps, canned food, birds, insects, squirrels, young rabbits, road kill remains and other carrion, fish, frogs, lizards, and the like, depending on the cat's surroundings and opportunities for hunting.

Well-fed house cats often hunt more than they will eat afterward. Because hunting drains a lot of strength from the body, this behavior is a pure waste of energy, something a wild animal could not

**It isn't likely that this cat is interested in the colossal bird on the television screen. It's just that every movement that catches the cat's eye gets its attention and, given a receptive emotional state, can stimulate the hunting instinct.**

# THE HUNTER AND THE HUNTED

**Whoever leaves a set table unsupervised is asking for trouble. Cats actually learn very quickly and easily that the dinner table is taboo, but will never understand as long as they live why a no-no should also apply when the authority figure is out of the way. Containers covered by lids or foil that exude tempting aromas don't present much of a problem for resourceful cats.**

afford. Cats cared for by people, however, don't need to concern themselves about their energy levels and use every opportunity to vent their hunting urge on prey.

Animals that stink or exude bitter secretions—and so taste bad—are caught by many cats and most often even killed, only to be dismissed and left. The most common of such bitter prey are toads, June bugs, spiders, shrews, and moles. Apartment and indoor cats often develop into ambitious fly hunters—and many devour an expertly hooked house fly afterward. Catch as catch can.

## How can a cat be kept from hunting birds?

If you have hung bird-houses in the yard, or if you know about nests in certain trees, you can cordon off the tree trunks with barbed collars or pine boughs. Many people put a bell around their cat's neck, which is supposed to give the birds a better chance of noticing the cat in time. The success rate of a belled cat is guaranteed to drop, even if it's only because the cat itself is irritated by the tinkling sound and therefore can't concentrate on the business at hand. In the end, I'm afraid the only way you'll completely stop a cat from hunting birds is to remove any and all opportunity by placing it under strict house arrest.

Cats are skillful hunters and fishers, at the kitchen table, too!

And for whom, pray, was the table so appetizingly set?

## The Business of Killing Birds

The subject of catching birds is a ticklish issue with many cat lovers. First, they themselves don't like seeing their cats murder cute little chirping birds; second, dead birds are often most annoying for the neighbors, who might for their part be bird lovers rather than cat lovers. It is certain that all cats like to hunt birds just as much as they like to hunt mice. It is just that birds are incomparably more difficult for them to catch, and therefore, experienced cats out in the country more or less give up on hunting birds. It's different in the city and in larger urban areas.

The ratio of birds to the combined number of other prey is obviously higher in urban than in rural areas. This is not surprising since there is generally a dearth of small rodents in cities nowadays. To vent their hunting urges, these cats are virtually forced to stick to birds; however, they catch almost exclusively sick, old, or very young birds. (As far as some varieties of songbirds go, as cruel as this sounds, three-quarters of the brood must die to keep the population in an area stable, and thus healthy. This is a fact fanatic bird protectors prefer to ignore.) In over fifty extensive ecological studies, not a single case of house cats jeopardizing any local bird species has yet been proven. It should be mentioned that this applies in mainland situations only. House cats that have access to small lake islands or bird cliffs can definitely present a serious threat to existing bird populations.

## Specialists in the Acquisition of Food

Cats are multitalented and learn extremely quickly, especially when it concerns ways of getting something to eat. For example, there are skillful anglers among them. On the bank of a fish pond or stream, the cat lies in wait for a fish to come close to the surface at the water's edge. In a flash, it dips its paw into the water, angles for the fish with claws extended, and slings it out in an arc over its shoulder onto dry land. In the same instant, the cat turns and pounces on its flopping prey, the way it would pounce on a mouse.

There are even credible reports of outdoor cats that regularly dig up earthworms in flower beds and eat them. City cats gone wild learn to open trash cans or plunder waste containers in covered street markets. The skill of cats' paws is almost limitless in the domestic arena as well. Containers that exude tempting aromas must be shut very tightly to keep out a cat that is seriously interested in the contents.

# EATING AND DRINKING

Our cat is a marked meat-eater. As a tireless hunter, it needs the high proportional protein of animal fare to have adequate energy for its demanding way of life. The greatest part of its need for liquids is satisfied by its meat diet. If a cat does feel thirsty, however, it quenches its thirst with water.

The natural diet of a free-ranging cat—and how could it be otherwise?—is the prey it hunts. Usually it brings the animal it has killed to a place where it can be relatively safe from unexpected disturbances and sets down to its meal there.

## Eating Prey

As a rule, cats crouch down when they start feeding. Only small morsels, such as fat insects, are sometimes swallowed while standing up. Cats always begin to eat furry animals from the head back, that is, in the direction of the fur. Feathered prey are also usually eaten from front to back. Most cats are in the habit of plucking birds, especially those the size of a blackbird, before consumption. The unwieldy tail and flight feathers, in particular, would certainly spoil the cat's enjoyment. Whether the job of plucking is performed in a cursory fashion or very carefully depends on the habits of the individual cat and on the degree of its hunger at the time. Whatever its approach, it pins the bird down to the ground with its forepaws while plucking out the feathers with its teeth. Every once in a while, the cat shakes its head fiercely to flick off the feathers sticking to its snout and it frequently licks its flanks. When it does this, it isn't cleaning its fur with its tongue in the normal way; it's wiping its tongue on its fur to clean off the downy feathers. After the meal of bird is over, only the plucked feathers—along with the legs and beaks of larger birds—are left lying around. Smaller birds are often swallowed whole.

Most often mice and other furry little prey are polished off in a similar manner—skin, hair, and all—while the cat might leave the skull of a young rabbit (large in cat proportions), and the long-haired fur along a rat's back is often regurgitated. Many cats tear the intestines out of the abdominal cavity and eat them as if they were a particular delicacy.

Cats don't chew their food up into mush before swallowing it, as we do. With their sharp premolars, which operate like a kind of crushing shears (see the chapter "Origin and Species"), they simply cut up their prey and then swallow the pieces whole. Because its premolars are located on the side of the upper jaw and the prey is on the ground, when it is eating its food, the cat tilts its head, chewing side toward the ground. The tilted position of the head is typical of a cat feeding. The jaw muscles are obviously put under a lot of pressure when it chews, as the cat frequently changes the side on which it is eating. The meat that sticks to big bones that are too thick to crunch up is gnawed off with the little incisors or scraped off with the cat's rough tongue. Smaller bones are just

**Cats that know each other well can usually arrange themselves to feed from a communal food dish if necessary; however, for a relaxed, stress-free meal, each cat should have its own bowl.**

crunched up and swallowed; the cat's particularly strong digestive juices will dissolve them.

Even though a ravenous cat is capable of devouring a mouse completely in less than two minutes, this is not what usually happens. As a rule, a cat exhibits neither greed nor haste during its meal, providing it feels safe in its feeding place and isn't disturbed. Often it will allow a few longer pauses now and again.

A concluding and thorough cleaning, especially of face and paws, is, for the tidy cat, a matter of course.

## How and when to feed?

As with us humans, the nutritional needs of cats vary greatly from individual to individual. Your cat is receiving the proper balance of food when it neither grows thin nor gets flabby pouches. The only way to find out is through trial and critical observation.

In principle, offer food at body or room temperature. Chunks of meat that are too cold will often be regurgitated immediately. This is not actually a serious health problem for the cat, but it means you will have a problem cleaning carpets. Canned food remains, in particular, leave vicious stains on many fabrics that are virtually non-fading and colorfast.

Feed your cat at least twice a day, preferably in the morning and evening. If the cat's meals are organized to coincide with your breakfast and supper, begging at the dinner table can be prevented. And please stick to somewhat regular feeding times. Cats happen to be even worse creatures of habit than people.

## The Balanced Diet

Food supplies all the materials that are essential to the growth and maintenance of the body. This holds true of the cat just as it does for all other animals, including people. In its prey, the cat finds all the nutritional substances it needs prepackaged, as it were, in small portions. Muscle, innards, and bones don't just supply protein and fat, but also vitamins and minerals in the right proportions. When a cat consumes a mouse, it even gets a plant or vegetable supplement, as it also eats the contents of the mouse's intestine and stomach.

The majority of cats today no longer sustain themselves on mice and other prey, but live in the comfortable land of plenty with human families. Here people bear the burden of ensuring that the diet of their four-footed friends nurtures their development in a healthy and balanced fashion. Innumerable varieties of kitchen recipes and menus for a proper feline diet circulate among owners and breeders. Equally varied is the selection of processed food available on the market today.

An entire industry employing veterinarians, nutritionists, behaviorists, researchers, and cooks is engaged in the search for new information on the feeding of house cats. This is how the bases for new food products are continually being established. In England, one of the largest of these research centers is housed in an old manor in the county of Leicestershire. All the latest varieties of experimental foods are fed to the three hundred cats that live here, surrounded by video cameras, scales, computers, and cooks. The twentieth generation of cats fed exclusively on processed food lives here today, and all of them are enjoying the best of health. In the United States, this type of experimentation is pursued by private industry.

As a by-product, as it were, of all the carefully controlled observations and metabolic

**Cats are meat-eaters that cannot disguise their predatory natures (ABOVE RIGHT). With sharp-sided lateral premolars, the cat cuts up its prey (BELOW LEFT). Horny papillae, aimed toward the back, make the cat's tongue rough like a file so that the cat can lick up liquid (BELOW RIGHT) and scrape meat fibers off large bones (ABOVE LEFT).**

**A cat cannot simply suck liquid into its mouth like many other animals. It uses its broad, flat tongue like a spoon and laps up small amounts into its mouth.**

# EATING AND DRINKING

analyses, biologists have made some interesting discoveries:

Given the opportunity, cats are "snackers." They will visit their food dish to eat up to thirty-six times within a twenty-four-hour period. Transferred to the natural outdoor setting, this would be a mouse here, a beetle there . . .

Cats prefer their food at 98 to 100 degrees Fahrenheit (37 to 38 degrees Celsius), which is what their body temperature is.

Cats are fussy eaters. For the ingredients in their meals,

they demand quality first. They may get bored and turn away from even the best dish if it is set out for them too often or exclusively. Then again, there are some cats that stubbornly insist on always having the same flavor to sink their teeth into. In fact, some of the leading veterinary nutritionists recommend not to change food often and to do so only gradually when a change is necessary.

In comparison with other meat-eaters, the cat needs a particularly high proportion of

protein in its diet for healthy development. A cat needs twice as much protein per pound of body weight as a dog.

All in all, however, cats taken care of by people require significantly less energy than self-sufficient hunters. That is why, besides high-energy fat and protein, their diet should also contain low-energy carbohydrates, for example, in the form of vegetable and cereal products. These vegetable and plant nutrients must first be released by cook-

ing or fermentation, otherwise the cat will not be able to digest them.

## Eating Grass

In contrast with many other kinds of predators, such as bears or foxes, cats do not eat fruit or other vegetable matter (besides what's in the stomachs and intestines of their prey). The only exception is the grass that all cats eat to a greater or lesser degree. They obviously don't graze like cows do, instead cats select one blade at a time by carefully sniffing and then, with head tilted to one side, they bite the tip off.

As to the reasons for their eating grass, at present we can only surmise, since we don't have conclusive results from scientific research on the subject. Very obviously, grass helps the cat to regurgitate hair swallowed while washing itself (also see the chapter "Cleanliness and Grooming"). Often cats will greedily swallow whole blades of grass following an extensive cleaning of the fur. The long blades of grass probably induce nausea, in much the same way as homemade remedies people have used as emetics. For cats that often pick at grass, the chewed blades pass through

**A truly noble pedigreed cat wants to receive its delicate entrée in a manner befitting its rank! For quite some time now, the cat industry has offered special dinnerware for cats with cat-minded designs, such as dishes with a mouse design that appears as the dish is emptied.**

## It shouldn't always be caviar!

The processed food available on the market today is healthy, completely satisfactory, and balanced for cats. It is also very practical because it makes the tiresome preparation of food unnecessary. This is not to say, however, that you should never give your cat anything fresh or raw anymore, though you need to be careful not to feed a cat food contaminated with bacteria. The best thing is to feed it a little of everything—canned food, dry food (keep sufficient drinking water available!), and fresh food, alternated regularly. Canned and fresh food should make up 20 percent of the cat's diet, while dry food makes up the remaining 80 percent. If the cat gets only canned food, its teeth and gums don't get used enough in the long run. Tartar build-up and gum disease can be the result. Here and there, something solid to sink its teeth into—for example, calf gristle, udder, or stomach—will prevent such "disorders of civilization."

Pork and poultry should be offered only if cooked. If these are offered raw, cats can ingest salmonellae, trichinae, and the virus causing pseudorabies (Aujeszky's Disease, which is ultimately fatal for cats). Most, but not all, cats think highly of innards (especially giblets) or fish on the menu occasionally. My tomcat categorically refuses liver, while his companion pounces on it each time, as if I had been letting her starve for weeks before that. Conversely, he is absolutely wild about fish, at which my lady merely turns up her nose. There is no arguing taste, even among cats.

*A propos* fish: Take the precaution of removing all the bones carefully. There are, it is true, lots of cats that consume fish they have caught themselves or "acquired" (or been given as a treat) at the pier, without having the slightest problem with bones, but you never know . . .

Finally, table scraps are not suitable cat food. Maybe Garfield is happy with lasagna, but your cat will only get fat. In the worst case, eczema, accompanied by loss of hair, can be the reaction to food that's too spicy.

their intestines quite normally without being digested. It is suspected that, as roughage, grass stimulates the operation of the intestines and thereby regulates digestion. Another possible hypothesis is that cats also instinctively fulfill their need for vitamins and trace elements by chewing grass.

**The way a cat lives determines to a large extent what it eats. While some luxury cats dine on lobster and shrimp, farm cats are hunting for a living and usually getting a daily "wage" of mice near the barn. Alley cats also search in trash cans and through garbage dumps for anything edible.**

# EATING AND DRINKING

## Water as a Thirst Quencher

Without water, there is no life and no cat life either! Yet cats get along with relatively little water. This is inherited from their forebears, who still inhabited the steppes and savannas. Their kidneys retain more water in the body than many other species.

A cat that feeds on prey absorbs a large part of its required water intake automatically, as it were, when it eats its kill. A mouse, for one, consists of up to 70 percent water. (The rest is protein, fat, bone, and gristle.) In raw muscle, the proportion of water is about 80 percent. If a cat feels thirsty, it will drink water from a stream or pond, from a puddle or watering can. Often it will even lick drops of rain or dew off plants. During hot summer days, of course, it needs to drink more than during cold, damp weather.

The tongue is an indispensable tool when it comes to drinking. Curled into a spoonlike shape, the tongue becomes a little ladle. With rapid flicks of the tongue, the cat laps liquid into its mouth. It can't simply suck up a drink the way other animals do.

Drinking can be much more important for cats that are fed by humans than for cats that take care of themselves. Canned food, also called wet food, still has about the same proportion of water as prey. But dry cat food, moist (dehydrated) nuggets, cat pellets (which are often freeze-dried), and much of whatever else is offered to cats in the way of delicacies and snacks, contain barely 10 percent water. This means that a cat on such a diet has to drink plenty of water.

One more thing on the subject of drinking. Milk, for a cat, is not a thirst-quenching drink but a liquid food substance. The cat's acidic stomach juices coagulate the consumed milk into solid bits of cheese that are heavy and take a long time to digest. Many cats are allergic to cow's milk, which contains different proteins from

### Do cats need grass?

Some cats often nibble on grass, others only very seldom. But every cat should have the possibility of doing so. A cat that can go outside helps itself in the nearest field or lawn as it sees fit. A house-bound cat has to be offered suitable grass in a flower pot or dish. Germinated wheat or oats are accepted as readily as the special "cat grass" sprouted in pet shops. (This is not to say that all cats like to eat every kind of grass equally well.) Set the indoor "lawn" in an easily accessible place, preferably in the vicinity of Fluffy's favorite spot, for instance, on a sunny windowsill. Cats that feel the urge to eat greens and can't find any grass will help themselves to any handy indoor plants. Unfortunately, they don't distinguish between easily and not easily digestible kinds. A number of house plants are distinctly poisonous, such as the poinsettia or the primrose, to name just a couple. Make sure that such varieties are not within reach of the cat, or make sure the cat doesn't have to rely on poisonous plants but can satisfy its need with suitable greens. Appropriate for cats' stomachs are the cypress grass and spider plants that are often found in many living rooms.

those found in cat's milk, and they react to it with diarrhea. Many, especially older, cats cannot absorb the plentiful sugars (primarily lactose) in their intestines. With these cats, too, diarrhea is the result. And finally, there are also cats that just won't accept proffered milk at all.

**Compared with other animals, cats can actually get along with relatively little water. However, especially on hot summer days or after longer physical exertion, they absolutely must take in sufficient liquid.**

**"When a cat eats grass, there will be a thunderstorm," the widespread farmers' saying goes.**

**Of course that saying is humbug. Grass aids digestion and helps the cat regurgitate hair it swallowed when cleaning itself. It is possible that, with the help of greens, it is also meeting a need for vitamins and minerals.**

**It's fun to drink from a running water faucet. Drops can be caught with the paw, too—a delightful game for many cats.**

# CLEANLINESS A

Cats are models of cleanliness. For hours they are busy each day, diligently licking their fur. Cats are also meticulous about cleaning and sharpening their claws. House-bound cats can be trained to bury their feces in a litter box. In free-ranging groups of cats, though, only socially inferior animals bury their excrement.

Without a doubt, cats are among the cleanest creatures in the world. This is certainly not the least of the reasons why they are such well-loved pets. In contrast with most other animals, they meet the hygienic requirements of even the most finicky owner.

## The Daily Care of Fur

You might have heard "With a lick and a promise," said colloquially when someone gives his or her face and body a hurried and all-too-cursory wash.

A less-fitting expression could hardly be found, for cats spend a third to half their waking hours grooming their fur. This sometimes amounts to more than three-and-a-half hours per day. And how thoroughly a cat undertakes this task! Here a tiny tuft of hair is smoothed down; there a matted spot is untangled. It removes dead hair and seeds from its fur, catches a flea, or removes encrusted dirt. It is completely engrossed in this occupation. The cat's main tool is its flat tongue, which is its washcloth, comb, and massage brush all rolled into one. Thanks to the cat's feline suppleness, it can reach almost all parts of its body with its tongue. Only for its head

and neck does the cat require the use of its forepaws, wetting them beforehand with its tongue. Tangles, encrusted fur patches, and parasites, it carefully nibbles with its little incisors.

Where the grooming of their fur is concerned, cats are as much individualists as they are in all other things. There are less thorough ones and particularly thorough ones, some that wash their forehead for hours and others that hardly ever use their paws for washing.

A contented cat lying in its basket, purring and patiently and diligently cleaning itself, inimitably radiates a feeling of coziness and calm.

# ND GROOMING

Its incredibly supple body and enormously mobile spine enable the cat to reach practically all parts of its coat with its tongue, which glides stroke by stroke over the fur like a rough washcloth.

The anus and genital opening are painstakingly cleaned. A cat with a soiled or encrusted rear end is certainly ill. Only obese cats or cats in advanced stages of pregnancy occasionally have difficulty, because of their portliness, in cleaning under their tails.

To help it wash its face and head, the cat uses its forepaws, which it thoroughly moistens beforehand with its tongue. Following each meal, an extensive cleaning of the snout is obligatory.

## Different Reasons to Wash

Of course, washing serves above all to keep the fur clean. Therefore, after a successful hunt and after eating from the food bowl, a thorough wash is dictated. The tongue loosens all kinds of dirt, as well as dead hair, from the fur. It also takes up essential vitamin D contained in the sebum in the coat. The sebaceous glands in the skin are stimulated by the licking to secrete oil, which impregnates the fur against moisture. The tongue massage also stimulates the growth of new hair. But washing means a lot more than all this for the cat: It improves cooling off, is used as a way to minimize embarrassment, and strengthens social contact as a mutually friendly gesture.

### Washing Instead of Sweating

A cat-wash is by no means a dry affair. As a cat washes, its tongue distributes a lickable amount of saliva over the fur. (Incidentally, it is this saliva that lends dry cat fur its typical, slightly sweet scent.) For cats, who do not have sweat glands distributed all over their bodies as we do (for more on this, see the chapter "Origin and Species"), saliva takes over the same function sweat does for us: It cools the cat, for as liquid evaporates, warmth is drained out of the body. The cooling function of washing also explains why cats lick more during hot weather, and why they usually lick themselves after exhausting activities such as hunting or playing. In summer, a cat's body loses as much liquid through this substitute sweating as it loses through urination. The cat must compensate for this by drinking.

### Washing out of Embarrassment

Cat owners know the following situation all too well. A cat meows at the door, waiting to be let out. You open the door, the cat rushes out, then it realizes it's raining in torrents. What now? The cat sits down and deliberately licks its flanks, as if there were nothing more pressing to be done at that moment. The way out of this situation—whether it stays out or comes back in—is still completely open. A cat often sits down and washes itself right in the middle of doing something. This means it is unsure of itself and undecided about what to do next. Through that noncommittal cleaning, it plays for time until it makes up its mind about the best way to proceed. We humans scratch our heads (originally also a cleaning gesture) or click a ball-point pen in and out when we don't quite know what we should say or do. In behaviorism, such displaced behavior, which has no logical connection to the situation at hand, is called a substitute activity or displacement activity. The pent-up drive to do something jumps over to another track, as it were, allowing the cat to relieve its tension in an unproblematic manner.

## Brushing and bathing a cat

A short-haired cat will undertake the grooming necessary to maintain its coat by itself—provided it is healthy. With the long-haired breeds this isn't the case. While humans have bred the long-haired coat, sufficiently increased grooming behavior was not bred along with it. Without help, long-haired cats usually cannot manage to keep their fur in immaculate shape, and it will get matted and dirty. If you have a long-haired cat, I strongly recommend a fifteen-minute fur grooming with a comb and brush every day.

Regardless, whether it is necessary for cleanliness or not, brushing is an ideal opportunity for regular contact between cats and humans and it should absolutely be allowed to become habit. With a short-haired cat, you should take the time to do this once a week. First, all cats enjoy their human friends devoting full attention to them. Second, you can prevent potential problems with swallowed hair. And third and finally, it offers an opportunity for a regular check-up for parasitic infestations, small wounds, or damage to the skin.

Although cats' fear of water is not exhibited as strongly as some people imagine (cats often play with water from faucets, catch fish from lakes and rivers, or are running around outside when it rains), most don't like bathing at all. Spare your cat regular baths to clean it! Brushing and a cat's tongue will normally gain the upper hand over any dirt in the fur. To treat skin aliments, baths in healing additives may become necessary from time to time. Let your veterinarian show you how best to proceed with this and which substances are appropriate.

**Mutual licking is customary, not only between a mother cat and her young or among littermates, but also among adult cats that have developed an intimate social bond. It is an unmistakably friendly gesture and, at the same time, an ever-welcome cleaning help for those hard-to-reach parts of the body.**

**Personal grooming is one of the main preoccupations of any cat.**

**A comfortable, warm spot, so perfect for a siesta! When it gets too warm, a little washing helps. The saliva distributed over the fur offers cooling through evaporation.**

**Long-haired cats need the help of humans to keep their coats clean and neat. Neither their grooming behavior nor the surface area of their tongue is prepared for fur whose proportions have been so altered by breeding.**

### Mutual Grooming

The first time every cat is licked is by its mother right after it is born. As early as three weeks, it begins to clean itself and, at the same time as washing its own coat, the kitten also begins to lick its littermates and mother. This natural care strengthens the social bonds in the little group. Mutual licking is also normal in adult cats that either grew up together or have developed a close social bond. A cat that licks another's fur says, unmistakably, "I like you." Above and beyond being a friendly gesture, this behavior is also an ever-welcome aid in grooming the parts of the body a cat has difficulty reaching. That is why, during mutual cleaning sessions, it is mostly the partner's neck, forehead, and ears that are given a good going over.

All cats obviously enjoy grooming, and at least a few fall into a gentle, pleasant purring. When the hand of a human friend strokes the fur like an oversized cat tongue, the best thing for a cat to do is to close its eyes and surrender itself completely to the enjoyment of the moment (for more on this, see the chapter "Understanding and Misunderstanding").

## Swallowed Hairs

When a cat licks its fur, it always swallows a large amount of loose hair. Much of this hair goes the "natural way" and is defecated. Since some of the hairs aren't digested, matted, elongated clumps of hair are always formed in the stomach and, sooner or later, are regurgitated. This is entirely normal, even if a cat lets out terrible noises while retching as if its last hour had come. No sooner is the hair ball lying in front of it than it regains its composure and ambles away indifferently.

If the cat has the opportunity to eat grass, this can facilitate vomiting (for more on this, see the chapter "Eating and Drinking"). This is especially important when the cat takes in particularly large amounts of hair, for instance, because it is molting, has particularly long fur, or is continuously cleaning itself because it is nervous. Should a hair ball get too big to be eliminated, the situation becomes critical. It will form an obstruction that may block the intestines. In the worst case, the veterinarian must operate to remove the clump of hair.

## Sharpening the Claws

Sharp, pointed claws are indispensable for a cat. It needs them for surefooted climbing, for grasping prey, and for defending itself effectively in fights. This is why the claws also get their turn in the daily cleaning procedure. With the front teeth, the cat nibbles out clinging dirt from between the toes and off the claws. To give them a final polish, the cat runs the claws of its forepaws one last time between its teeth, one by one, as if to tear each one out. But what good are sparkling clean claws when they've become dull? Not much. And because of that, again and again, we see a cat sharpening its claws. It does this by getting rid of the outer, worn-out claw husks. Out from underneath appears the latest growth of new and, at least in the case of the front paws, extremely pointed claws. It gets rid of the old husks on the back claws with its teeth, occasionally chewing them right off. To loosen the claw husks from the front claws, the cat prefers to dig its claws into soft wood and pull hard along the grain. Outside, the cat finds a tree trunk, if possible one with rough bark, an old wooden

**Having to attend to several things at once doesn't present any problem to cats. They happily lie down for a rest on an elevated lookout post and at the same time perform a portion of their daily grooming routine.**

# CLEANLINESS AND GROOMING

**To clean the claws of the forepaws, the cat nibbles away the dirt clinging to them with its little incisors, making it look as though the cat is actually biting its fingernails.**

**To sharpen its claws, the cat digs them into wood and strongly pulls down on them. In doing this, it sheds the old husks of the claws that have become dull, and from underneath the newly grown needle-sharp claws appear.**

**Cats like to use tree trunks with rough bark as a manicure aid.**

post, or even a fence board that is not too smooth. A cat that lives exclusively indoors needs a suitable substitute.

Just as washing doesn't serve only to clean the fur, sharpening the claws doesn't only serve as a manicure for a cat. Another important function is to practice extending and relaxing the claws and to strengthen the muscles needed to do that. Besides this, the scratches set out scent markers that mark a cat's territory (for more on this, see the chapter "At Home and on the Road"). A cat has sweat and scent glands on the balls of its feet, whose excretions during

## Homemade scratching things for indoor cats

On the pet store market, you can buy cat scratching posts and boards in multiple variations and in every price range. With a little bit of technical skill, you can also easily construct them. A cat will happily accept a thick wooden rod with clothesline made of hemp wrapped around it, a rough doormat tacked to the wall at cat height, or a thick branch or rough board clamped between floor and ceiling. For my cats, I covered a wooden board with a carpet remnant and leaned it against the windowsill on which they particularly like to sit. This way, they can not only scratch on it, but also reach their favorite spot comfortably.

scratching transmit the individual smell of a cat.

Lastly, sharpening claws is also a physical dominance gesture, as behaviorists call it. From long-term studies in the wild, we know that free-ranging cats sharpen their claws a lot more often in the presence of others of their kind than when they are alone. Dominant animals (both female and male) seek completely atypical spots from time to time. The main thing is they are being watched by inferior animals. Impressive behavior, therefore, is showing off in cat language! Only the humans in the house won't, as a rule, be terribly im-

pressed by all that scratching around. Generally they insist upon cats limiting themselves to the scratching-post provided for that purpose. In the vast majority of cases, this can be achieved with appropriate steady training measures (see the chapter "Playing and Learning").

In a few countries, especially in the United States, it was popular (and in part still is today) simply to remove the front claws of indoor cats. To prevent further growth, they are amputated along with the last joint of the toes. But since claws and the sharpening of claws are integral to a cat's

personality, such "adaptive measures" constitute not only physical, but psychological, mutilation of the cat. In Germany, Austria, and Switzerland, declawing is legally prohibited.

## Cleanliness in Urination

Emptying the bladder and bowel is, for the cat as for all other animals, a natural, commonplace function. The theme comes to the forefront only with cats that are kept indoors, for there people's (understand-

able) wishes are diametrically opposed to the needs of cats. Luckily, a compromise that is almost always acceptable to both sides can be found in the form of a litter box. Here, it is again evident how adaptable the cat is in its way of life, and how ready and willing it is to fit into the daily routine of its human friends. Only a small minority of cats are really mule-headed.

A free-ranging alley cat or farm cat doesn't use a fixed place to urinate or defecate. Nevertheless, in numerous observational studies, a series of feline "toilet rules" have been ascertained. Cats generally

**The claws of the hind paws are cleaned and cared for with the same meticulous precision as the front ones, even though they are not nearly as sharp.**

## Where to put the litter box?

Cats want to be undisturbed when they go about their "business." Therefore, place the litter box away from frequently used areas of the house. However, it must be easily accessible; sometimes cats, too, have to get to the toilet in a hurry! Place the litter box in the general vicinity of—but not too near—the usual eating spot.

It should, if possible, be at a good distance away from favored sleeping places. If two or more cats live together in a domestic group, they need at least two litter boxes; but even for a single cat, two "little spots" aren't an exaggerated luxury. Two litter boxes better accommodate their natural habit of using various urination and defecation places. Many veterinarians recommend having litter boxes numbering one more than the total number of cats. It is best to put them in different rooms.

The cat should be able to step into the box or tub without any trouble, and, once inside, be able to look out over the edge. The box should also be large enough that the cat can turn around inside it without being cramped for space. It should measure no less than twelve inches by sixteen inches (thirty by forty centimeters). As for litter, it is better to use a gravel cat litter from the pet supply store. Pet stores also carry a sand-based clumping litter, which is becoming increasingly popular. Materials like shredded paper, loose garden peat, or wood shavings are cheaper, it's true, but they make for incomparably more work. They fly farther afield when the cat is digging, or stick to its paws and then get spread all over the house.

Shake the litter out some one and one-half to two inches (four to five centimeters) deep and change it regularly—that is to say, at least twice a week—and remove the feces every day. The "bio" litter available on the market can be added to your compost pile, but remove the feces first. Recently, deodorized litter and perfumed cat boxes have also become available. Here, I would advise cautious restraint. Not all cats perceive these smells as pleasant.

don't urinate in the same place they dispose of their feces. And in no case is excrement disposed of in the proximity of sleeping places or customary eating places. While urine normally just seeps into the ground, feces are carefully buried by most cats. But not by all, though! They really don't do this from a need for hygiene, but much more as a sign of rank. Burying feces is typical of cats with inferior rank that seek thereby to prevent or reduce the spread of odor. Dominant cats, in contrast, leave their feces out in the open, as a kind of "scent threat," as if to say, "I was here and I am strong! Nobody better dare cross my path!" So that this message is communicated to as many cats possible, such despots usually deposit their feces in exposed, often even elevated, places.

The smell of excretions also functions as a calling card for cats, and it is obvious that they can recognize individual cats familiar to them (for this, also see the chapter "Understanding and Misunderstanding").

Cats are also very interested in the smells they themselves produce. As soon as they have done their "business," they sniff at it. While they are digging it under, they are in the habit of repeatedly sniffing it as well, quite possibly to check on the level of the smell.

The fact that house cats that share their houses with people are generally careful to bury their feces suggests they perceive people as domineer-

**From time to time, the business of washing has such a calming effect on the cat that it seems to forget everything—even to pull its tongue back into its mouth.**

ing "super cats." If young kittens are shown where they can find a litter box when they start stepping out of the nest, they learn effortlessly to use this as agreed. Also, when they arrive in a new house as young cats, they only need to be shown the appropriate place a few times before they catch on. Should the cat take up dirty habits, urinating or defecating near its box or in another part of the house, this behavior could be organically caused and attributable to a disease.

In most cases, however, it is just a behavioral disorder that can be traced back to human error in the lack of cleanliness of the provided litter box (see also the chapter "Illness and Age").

**A cat that doesn't hold an absolute dominant position on its home turf buries its feces deliberately. In loose topsoil, be it in the litter of the cat box or in the flower bed during the winter, it will dig a hole, perform its "business," and cover it carefully. Only highly valued and very self-assured cats, as a rule tomcats, will leave their feces uncovered as a provocative "scent threat."**

# SLEEPING AND DREAMING

Cats are true masters of the art of sleeping, spending a good portion of their day asleep. The sleeping place has to be warm and safe. You can tell by the position of the cat's body whether it is merely dozing, lightly slumbering, or deep within the realm of dreams.

**T**he sleeping cat is a symbol of pleasantly peaceful oblivion! Daintily curled up on soft pillows, pleasurably stretched out in sunny spots, or shyly hidden under cover protected from the wind and from sight, depending on the circumstances of life, cats spend hour upon hour sleeping and dozing.

## Champion Long Sleepers

Of all of cats' activities, sleeping is by far their favorite. On average, cats spend sixteen or more out of twenty-four hours sleeping, at least two-thirds of their time. For those of you who enjoy number games, by the end of its life, a twelve-year-old cat will have been awake for only four years at the most.

Most other mammals sleep a lot less than cats do. Only the opossum is known to sleep longer on average (eighteen hours daily), and some bats sleep for up to twenty hours at a stretch. Why just the cat sleeps so much is not known. Scientists have offered various hypotheses in the search for an explanation. One of them is that the higher an animal's energy needs are, the more useful are lengthy periods of rest in which the consumption of energy is reduced. A preda-

**A cat that has a hammock is really sitting pretty. Even if the thing is all over the place when you want to get in, it does let you sleep wonderfully and comfortably once you're there.**

tor always requires a lot of energy for hunting. Since the cat is a very successful hunter because of its perfect physical qualities, it saves a lot of time obtaining food, time that can be used to sleep. Another working hypothesis of sleep researchers suggests that an animal that is itself hunted by many natural enemies can afford only brief periods of inattention. Should the animal sleep too soundly, it will likely not survive long. Hunters, on the other hand, can per-

mit themselves a substantial amount of sleep without great exposure to danger. This holds especially true for those predators that can locate a sleeping lair inaccessible to natural enemies. (The wildcat, for example, likes to withdraw to a high-up tree hollow for this purpose.)

## Sleep Times

Cats have a fundamentally different sleep behavior than we people have. Where we normally sleep eight hours at a stretch, and that usually at

night, cats engage in a variety of shorter and longer naps throughout the entire day. Exactly when and for how long they sleep at any one time is difficult to say as no two cats are alike and one day is not like another. Daily sleep routines may be influenced by any or all of the following: weather,

activity of its human companions, the age of the cat, its physical condition, relative degree of hunger or satiety, and, not least, by the intensity of its current sexual interests. Cats tend to sleep a lot on cold or rainy days. Young and very old cats obviously sleep more than healthy adults. An empty

# SLEEPING AND DREAMING

stomach is definitely cause to awaken. And when love interests present themselves there is a lot of action; a male or female can feasibly skip a series of naps.

Cats that live in a close-knit community of people are surprisingly adaptable in their daily rhythms. Cats that are alone a lot, especially cats belonging to working people, seek social contact when their owners are at home and have time for them. They generally sleep through the hours of being alone. Whether the cat's owner is an early bird or a

**Cats seek out spots that seem suitable for a little nap very carefully—a sunny balcony, where potted plants offer a little cover and, as required, some shade; a softly upholstered chair (such a practical piece of furniture people couldn't possibly have invented for themselves alone!); or a warm, somewhat elevated corner in the backyard, where you can dream the day away undisturbed.**

night owl, the cat adapts its daily rhythms accordingly.

Cats have maintained certain innate "wild" patterns of behavior, however. Almost all cats are up and around at daybreak. The free-ranging cat starts the day with a prowl or survey of its territory, the indoor cat wanders through rooms, and the cat that can go out makes a brief excursion outdoors. Cats become even more active in the early evening hours. In line with their wild heritage, cats are typical twilight predators. This means they usually go off to hunt at the onset of twilight. Indoors this inherited behavior often expresses itself in wild, unruly games of pursuit, daredevilish climbing excursions, and jogs down the hallway. When the urge to move has diminished, many a cat immediately slips in one more little nap before it turns to its customary evening cuddling ritual with people.

## Sleeping Places

A cat is particular when it comes to choosing a place to sleep. Above all, it has to be warm and free from drafts. If possible, it should also be somewhat hidden away and preferably somewhere high up. The wildcat in the forest likes to seek out a sleeping place in the hollow of a big old tree trunk as far off the ground as possible. Places that cats select indoors for their dream hours sometimes seem pretty strange to us. It doesn't always have to be a soft pillow or a cozy corner on the sofa (although these can be very attractive snoozing places!); a hard windowsill below which a heater pleasantly spreads warmth rates even higher. The ventilation grill in the refrigerator through which the waste heat rises may become the house tom's favorite spot. The main thing is, it's warm! For

**Kittens love to snuggle! It doesn't just keep them warm when they sleep, but also gives them a calming feeling of security, just like being in the nest with their mother.**

the cat, a warm sleeping place means it can keep its energy consumption to a minimum. It does not cost it any metabolic calories to keep its body at an even temperature.

The feline predilection for warm spots goes so far that many a cat owner has smelled the odor of singed fur when their cat has dozed off too close to the open hearth. Cat fur is such a good insulator that the immense radiant heat of the fire doesn't reach the skin underneath.

Cats are passionate sun worshippers. In familiar territory—inside the house, outside in the controlled environment of the yard, or higher up on the roof of a shed or house—they take advantage of every patch of sunlight. When the sun shifts and moves along the ground, the cat moves with it. Experienced cats can do so without fully waking. Only on the hottest days of summer will a cat prefer to sleep in the

shade. Then it withdraws from the dazzling sun under a hedge or in the semi-shade of a perennial border.

## Sleep Isn't Just Sleep

For several decades scientists have made it their mission to investigate those processes that occur during sleep—in the body and specifically in the brain. For these studies, that phlegmatic beast, the cat, is a particularly appropriate subject. We are, therefore, more informed about the sleep of cats than that of any other creature, with the exception of humans.

Sleep is, mind you, by no means the state of complete rest it was long taken to be. Rather, the brain keeps working constantly, both during waking and sleeping states. With an electroencephalograph (EEG), the brain activity

## A bed for the cat, quickly and easily made

A cat likes to seek out its sleeping place in the house for itself. Most often a cat has two or three favorite places where it regularly lies.

By offering your cat a real cat "bed" in a warm place, sheltered from drafts and, if possible, somewhat hidden away, you can persuade almost any cat to sleep in the place you have selected for it.

It need not, by any means, be an expensive cat basket, although there are many available on the market in all styles and fashions imaginable. A simple

sturdy cardboard box is just as suitable. Just make sure it's large enough that the cat can stretch out to its full length in it. You can make the box comfortable for the cat by putting a thick layer of newspaper on the bottom with a folded blanket on top of it. You can easily change this bedding when it needs to be washed. My own cats like to sleep on a rustic-style sheep's wool rug. Just one more thing. Cats sleep because they need the rest. You should respect this and leave them alone while they are sleeping.

**A soft, warm sheepskin is the kind of bedding of which a cat can only dream. In falling asleep its head slowly sinks down onto its paws (LEFT).**

**The cat has now slipped from the first phase of light sleep into a deep sleep. Its muscles are totally relaxed; its body lies completely limp. It is now very difficult to wake up (CENTER LEFT).**

**While short deep sleep phases are still alternating with periods of light sleep, the cat keeps changing its position (CENTER LEFT; CENTER RIGHT).**

**A cat looks particularly cute when it is lying there all curled up, resting on the back of its head with one paw delicately covering its nose, or even its eyes—a position preferred by many cats (RIGHT).**

of a sleeper can be directly measured and plotted. To do this, tiny electrodes are painlessly attached to the scalp. They receive the weak electrical impulses that are produced by the activity of the nerve cells in the brain. The impulses are then processed through an oscillograph and transmitted by galvanometric pens to a read-out on graph paper. The various curves and peaked lines on the graph paper are interpreted by sleep researchers to provide information on the quality and intensity of a subject's sleep.

It has been demonstrated that the sleep activity of cats (as well as that of people and of most other mammals that have been subjects of research) is characterized by two typical patterns of brain activity. Whereas the EEG reading of a cat in a waking state shows

small, tightly packed irregular peaks, the reading produced by a dozing or lightly sleeping cat is characterized by long, irregular waves on the graph. Mostly the cat lies there, head raised and forepaws tucked under the chest. However, the cat sometimes falls asleep in a sitting position. If this happens, the muscles of the body maintain their tension and the cat is stiff and motionless. This kind of sleep is called restful sleep or, after the accompanying brain waves, slow-wave sleep. It is a light sleep from which a cat can easily waken. This phase lasts fifteen to thirty minutes, during which time the head relaxes, the body stretches out, and the cat rolls onto its side. As this is happening, the corresponding patterns on the EEG change. When the cat slips from a light to a deep sleep, the peaking lines on the EEG become smaller and closer together. Not quite as close together or as irregular as in the waking state, but, all in all, brain activity in deep sleep is astoundingly similar to the brain activity of a cat when it is awake; however, during deep sleep the muscles relax and the cat is limp. Now the cat is quite difficult to arouse. Small wonder that sleep researchers have referred to this state as paradoxical sleep. Another term used is quick sleep, as it is characterized by rapid movement of the brain waves. On average, the deep sleep phase in a cat lasts only six minutes and is followed by a phase of lighter sleep. The tension in the cat's muscles increases again (although you can't usually see this happening) and the cat, if undisturbed, remains comfortably stretched out sideways. Periods of light and heavy sleep alternate until waking.

## Cat Dreams

A telling feature of deep sleep in mammals is the occurrence of small rapid eye movements. These rapid eye movements (REM) have supplied a designation for the deep sleep state, known also as REM sleep. The quick movements of the eyeballs behind closed or partially closed lids can be seen, even without technical equipment. Experiments conducted on human subjects that were woken from an REM sleep state have established that REM sleep is the phase of sleep in which dreams occur.

Of course, we cannot know with certainty if a cat is dreaming during the REM sleep phase, and we can only speculate about the nature or content of any such dreams. The obvious

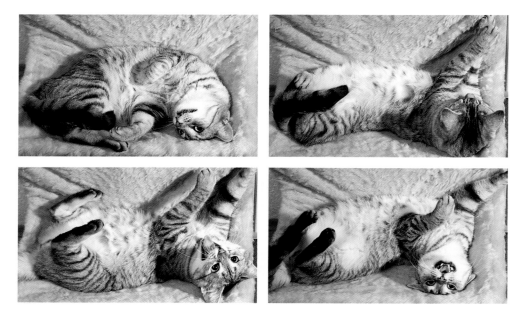

**Typical stretching exercises after waking up (drawings).**

**When cats wake up from a long sleep (ABOVE LEFT), they usually stretch extensively (ABOVE RIGHT; BELOW). This loosens up the joints and** gets the circulation going again. That's how you ready yourself for whatever the day may bring.

and substantial impediment to knowing about the dreams of cats is that they cannot provide verbal responses to sleep researchers. However, anyone who has observed a sleeping cat would be hard pressed to question the reality of the existence of cat dreams: The paws twitch, the tip of the tail swishes back and forth, the whiskers vibrate, the ears turn, and the jaw chatters, as if the cat were experiencing different scenes from its daily life. And all these motions and twitches happen in a body that is otherwise completely limp.

Why do animals dream? What purpose do dreams serve? We don't know. However, it would appear that REM sleep serves some important biological function: If an individual is deprived of REM sleep by being purposely woken up, hallucinations and thought disorders soon develop. Dream researchers have discovered that the more highly developed the brain of the species, the longer the REM phases are and the more significant dream activity is. Whereas no such phases are yet known in fish and reptiles, birds have REM sequences of a minute, rats have sequences lasting up to thirty minutes per day, and humans have sequences lasting from one and one-half to two hours per day. However, the cat exceeds them all, spending up to three hours daily in REM sleep.

## Waking Up

At the sound of an alarming noise, a sleeping cat can be on its feet instantly, alert and ready for action. This reaction harks back to the primal heritage of a wild animal intent on survival. When a cat surfaces undisturbed from a long restful sleep, however, it makes quite a ceremony of waking up. In slow-motion tempo the eyelids open (a rapid blink would be beneath a cat's dignity), the head raises up. This is followed by a long hearty yawn, so wide it looks as though the cat is going to dislocate its jaw. It doesn't just get up, it rises, again in slow-motion. Now come obligatory stretching exercises to loosen stiff limbs and get the circulation going again. These exercises are almost always done in the same sequence. First, the forelegs are stretched out way forward. Then, the back is first flexed into a concave curve, then arched into the classic cat humpback. Finally, the cat takes two or three steps forward that stretch the hind legs backward one after the other. That is the routine. Most cats now sit down and start washing themselves, either to comb fur crumpled from sleeping back to silky smoothness or simply to gain time while deciding on the next activity of the day.

**Ah, how deliciously lazy a cat's life can be!**

# LUST AND LOVE

Cats have a reputation for having a pretty free and easy love life. The annual peak period for this activity is about February. When a male encounters a female, they approach one another gradually in the course of quite a complicated courtship ritual. The decision whether and when it will come to mating is always up to the female. Often several suitors court her, yet the female knows most definitely which of them appeals to her. This won't always be the strongest or the most handsome one, and likely won't be the same one every evening, either.

For centuries, the cat has been a symbol of sex and fertility. This won't surprise anyone who has had the chance to watch feline love in action. Hardly any other animal makes its intimate life as public as cats do. Their longing for the opposite sex can neither be overlooked nor ignored.

## Love Songs and other Cat Music

On suburban front lawns, in backyards, and everywhere else cats live, they can go at it pretty loudly some nights. The passionate and vociferous tones from all those cat throats have, no doubt, made many a person lose a well-deserved night's rest. A bucket of water thrown out the window into the darkness of the night seldom hits its mark and results in little more than a few minutes of suspenseful silence before the next "verse" is taken up. Generally, all that "cat music" is lumped together and taken to be the love songs of tomcats— a widespread misconception. When the feline rutting season reaches its peak, twice a year from mid-January to about the beginning of March and again in a less intense form during June or July, fights among toms are particularly frequent. Their threatening battle yowls can rise to a screeching *fortissimo* when the fight gets serious. Feline love songs, quiet and alluring, sound totally different, and are engaged in equally by both males and females. They croon and purr, mew and meow with overwhelming ardor, often for hours at a time. The German poet Victor von Scheffel called it "a sound that can make stones cry and drive people crazy."

## The Amorous Female

The female cat usually sexually matures at six to nine months and no later than one year of age. Siamese females are often precocious and are already calling for toms when they are six months old. A rutting female cat is said to be "in heat" or "in season," and anyone who has ever seen this condition certainly won't ask where the term came from. Most veterinarians have received worried phone calls precipitated by a female cat that supposedly has cramps and is rolling around on the floor in pain. When she also appears

**Only after long, patient courtship does the female cat allow the tom to mount her. The actual act of mating lasts only a few seconds.**

**A cat in heat rolls on the floor with abandon. In between times she rubs her head and flanks on all kinds of objects to leave her scent marks. No tomcat can overlook such promising overtures (ABOVE). When the female is finally ready to mate, she presents the tom her genitals by hollowing her back, raising her hindquarters, and lifting her tail to the side. This position is an unmistakable invitation to the chosen male to mount her. By gently applying pressure on top of the cat's lower back with your hand, you can readily ascertain what stage of the cycle she is in (RIGHT-HAND PAGE). If she is ready to mate, she responds to this pressure with an "inviting pose."**

## What's to be done with a cat in heat?

A cat in heat doesn't just call for a tom, she also wants to go to him. Don't underestimate the obstinacy and resourcefulness a cat can muster when she wants to slip out. Many cat owners do not even try to keep their cats locked in at this time. They often won't succeed anyway. In a careless moment, some door is bound to be left open a crack . . .

Even if you do succeed in keeping her inside and have survived with your nerves somewhat intact, don't celebrate too soon. In two to three weeks the whole performance can begin all over again. A cat whose needs are never satisfied can even, on rare occasions, turn into a cat that is morbidly in heat all the time. If that happens, the whole story will become an agony not just for you, but for the cat as well.

So, if you don't want to have a litter of kittens in the house with unfailing regularity, the only permanent solution is to have your female cat spayed. Most veterinarians and humane societies strongly recommend this procedure because of the large number of unwanted kittens born each year. (They also recommend neutering male cats.) When a cat is spayed, the veterinarian removes the cat's ovaries and uterus. This operation results in infertility. It also means that the cat will no longer "roll around" in heat, or at most, only in passing.

Incidentally, the "pill for cats" is at best a temporary solution, for instance, when a breeding queen shouldn't become pregnant for a while. Administered for a longer period of time, this hormonal treatment can lead to inflammation of the uterus.

restless, hardly eats, constantly utters strange sounds, and is generally behaving in a pretty bizarre fashion, the diagnosis is usually obvious. The cat is, very simply, in heat.

However, rolling around on the floor isn't the only way the female makes evident her longing for a tomcat. She chirrups and coos, "chats" talkatively, or calls out in a plaintive, monotonous voice for a passing feline gentleman to hear her. She will rub her head and flanks up on anything in her path—on stones, posts, doorjambs, furniture, people's legs. With her back hollowed, hind end up, tail held to the side, she will present her backside. And then she will roll around some more—and then some more.

As it is with the character of cats in general, the behavior of each female is clearly individual and distinct when she is in heat. There are reserved, rather timid ladies that turn into male-hungry maniacs, and calm, even-keeled (often older and more experienced) females whose "time" can hardly be noticed. (The toms in the neighborhood do notice, of course. After all, they are toms, and they have a good nose for this sort of thing.) With temperamental cats, being in heat can develop into a veritable natural phenomenon.

If she becomes pregnant and has two litters, a free-ranging female normally goes into heat twice a year and her season lasts eight to ten days, although she is actually ready to mate for only three to four days. If she does not find a tom to couple with her during this time, she can come into season again every three to four weeks until fall. But even here, there are large individual differences. There are cats that come into heat only every couple of months, even when they haven't mated, and in extreme cases, come into heat only twice a year. Persian queens are well known for this.

In nature, the readiness of female cats to reproduce is controlled by the length of the day. From October on, when the days are growing noticeably shorter, feline love takes an extended break. Babies born during the winter have little chance of survival. Under experimental conditions, this wintertime hiatus can be shortened or done away with altogether by turning on additional artificial lights. Then, even farm cats will come into season again as early as November (instead of February). House-bound cats that live with a regular cycle of twelve to fourteen hours of light per day can come into season at any time of the year.

## The Sexual Activities of Tomcats

Puberty in young toms lasts a relatively long time. Production of the male sex hormone testosterone, which controls the maturing of the sex organs as well as typical tomcat mating behavior, starts when the tomcat is just four months old.

At the age of six to eight months, some toms are already eagerly "practicing" with every female cat they can find, just to get a feel for it. It is usually not

# LUST AND LOVE

A tomcat has all kinds of things to do to keep his range in order and always be up to date on the rutting conditions of the females there. When he tracks down a female in heat, he finds it effective to advertise his presence through frequent scent marking. By spraying urine on various landmarks (ABOVE), the tomcat ensures his rivals remember him, and the marks attest to his entitlement to the female population in this area. When actually encountering a female cat, the tomcat is exceedingly eager to smell her backside (CENTER). The more obviously she smells of being in heat, the more stubbornly he dogs her heels as a suitor. If he loses sight of her for too long, another tom may well snatch her away, literally right out from under his nose. On the other hand, if he is too rash and approaches her too insistently, she will brusquely let him know that she isn't yet ready for an amorous adventure. The claws of an infuriated female speak a language that's all too clear.

until their ninth or twelfth month, though, that they manage to couple successfully. Free-ranging toms first have their chance when they are three to four years old and have acquired a sufficiently high standing in the community of toms that they are no longer shut out of the competition for the females.

Sexually mature males are ready for amorous adventures year-round, but they are not always as keen as they are when spring is getting underway. Driven by restlessness, they roam far afield, always on the lookout for the irresistible scent of a female in heat. They won't come home for nights on end. Territorial boundaries are suddenly ignored and "fraternities" (see the chapter "At Home and on the Road") are temporarily canceled. Even before a female is actually sighted, there will be numerous fights among the local toms. These are to clear up relations and standings among the males beforehand, as it were.

To deliberately underline their presence, rutting toms distribute their personal calling cards in the form of sprays of urine. They spray everywhere it appears strategically meaningful to them. Secretions from

## What to do about a tom's scent on doorways and furniture

Different methods of handling this problem range in effectiveness. Cleansing agents or deodorants available on the market don't help much. But products are available that break down the components of urine. These can be effective. You might also be able to moderate the smell with diluted vinegar. A few drops of lemon oil in water will also cover up the tom's perfume somewhat.

Although the spraying habits of tomcats vary, it must be said that 99 percent of all uncastrated toms spray to advertise their presence. The only way to stop this is castration (and the results aren't guaranteed even then).

The best thing is to have the cat neutered before he is completely sexually mature. This not only suppresses his sex drive right from the start, but also his urge to spray. If you wait until later before delivering him to go under the veterinarian's knife, he will probably already have developed the characteristically wide head of a tom and possibly won't ever completely lose his sexual interests, including his tiresome habit of spraying everywhere.

By the way, when you share your home with a female cat, and one day notice that typical marking scent, don't suspect your neighbor's tom right off. Although it's unlikely, you might be doing him an injustice. Sometimes it suddenly occurs to females as well to distribute such aromatic calling cards in their surroundings. Mind you, her perfume isn't quite as pungent as his.

the anal glands mix with the urine to give the spray an amply pungent scent of the "Predator House" variety. Since many tomcats abstain from this kind of self-expression in the close quarters of their own homes and prefer to place their marks in the neighborhoods of female cats, this activity affects the owners of female cats more than it does the owners of males. A few

**The urine of a cat in heat has a particularly interesting fragrance for the sensitive feline nose. The tomcat carefully investigates the spot in question.**

# LUST AND LOVE

When the tom and female live together, it is always easier for him to maintain control over her readiness to mate. In the "critical days" he pursues her often, wherever she goes, and smells by the scent of her genitalia what stage of her season she is in (ABOVE).

Many tomcats behave like Romeos in love during the days of their courtship. They not only constantly seek out the proximity of the female to keep an eye on her, but also play, snuggle, and flirt affectionately with her (CENTER). This is in no way guarantees, though, that the female, when things finally "get serious," won't suddenly prefer some other tomcat who happens to turn up. Very few females show a feeling of fidelity to a partner. If they have the opportunity to do so, most mate with several toms when they are fully in heat. When a female cat presses herself flat to the floor with hindquarters raised and tail held to the side, it is an unmistakable expression of her mating mood (BELOW). The request really couldn't be any clearer, now, could it?

toms, though, stubbornly feel they have to perfume their own favorite places in the house as well.

Once the tom has tracked down a female in heat, he visits regularly. He eagerly investigates the smell of the urine she has deposited, waits patiently for the female to appear, calls to her—in brief, he stays alert.

## The Feline Wedding

Most often several tomcats court a female in heat. With cats—as with most mammals, incidentally—the principle of

females' choice rules. The female certainly does not always opt for the strongest, showiest, most muscle-bound, or sexiest of her suitors. Often her choice falls on some wimpy, shy, or particularly shabby tom. She knows her own mind on such matters.

Every tom takes a slightly different approach in his efforts to win a lady's favor. The most important thing for him to remember is that if he approaches her too quickly, he runs the risk that she will either flee or greet him with hisses and slaps of the paw. Each female also has her own "tricks" in the mating game. Most respond to males' advances with so-called quick rushes, where the female runs a short distance, then sits down and lures the tom on with crooning and soft calls. A tried-and-true tactic of experienced toms consists of first waiting a while a little to one side until the female's attention wanders and she looks away. Then he hurries a few steps closer. If the female unexpectedly turns her head back in his direction, he plays the disinterested, just-happened-to-be-in-the-neighborhood-by-sheer-coincidence role, sits down, looks off into space, and even washes himself. This little game repeats itself until the female is within reach. If no obvious rejection is forthcoming from her side, the tom leaps over to her, grabs the fur on the nape of her neck with his teeth, and mounts her. Some females don't need to be so precipitously overpowered, but instead offer themselves to the tom voluntarily, their backs hollow and their backsides raised up.

The tomcat's grip on the back of the cat's neck makes her stand still while they couple. (This is the same reflex that makes young cats go limp when their mother picks them up by the scruff of the neck.) The tom takes the female between his forelegs and tries to find her genital opening with his erect penis. Actual mating

**It is not unusual for cat couples to exhibit a touching affection, especially when the animals know each other well. They behave, in fact, like teenagers in love, not overlooking any chances to exchange caresses or simply to be close to each other. Among cats that have free access to the outdoors, the same "lover" may return during mating season year after year.**

# LUST AND LOVE

**Scenes of feline love. When the female finally allows the tom to approach her at the peak of her season, everything happens very quickly. The tom takes the female, who is crouched in front of him with her backside raised up, between his legs, grabs her by the back of the neck with his teeth, and enters her with quick thrusts to accomplish the mating act. The concluding withdrawal of the penis is quite painful for the female. Generally, she will utter a brief cry and turn very aggressively on the tom. But then, after a few minutes, the female is usually ready for "another round" (drawing).**

takes only a few seconds. No sooner is it over, than the female lets out a loud cry and turns on the tom, usually very aggressively. If he doesn't withdraw at once, she attacks him, hissing and swinging at him with her paws. The reason for this sudden change in mood is the short barbs that slant

backward on the tom's penis. On withdrawal, they painfully tear the walls of the female's vagina. It is supposed that they provide strong stimulation of the vagina to trigger ovulation in the female.

Suddenly the female sits down and starts licking the area around her genitals. A

few short minutes after copulation, she will once again be ready to mate.

Most females will go with various toms one after the other. This means the kittens in a single litter may have different fathers. A female may also grant only one tom her favor over an extended period of time, even if there is no lack of other interested suitors.

With partners that already know each other very well, mating occurs much more quietly, calmly, and easily. The female crouches in front of the tom in the mating position and looks at him invitingly over her shoulder. He mounts her—most often without biting her neck—and accomplishes his mission.

**It is a mistaken belief that cats mate only in the dark of night. Provided he is on familiar turf and feels sure of himself, a tom who is after a female in heat and can tell by her demeanor that she will tolerate his intimate advances isn't going to bother about whether it's light or dark out—or about two- or four-legged onlookers that might be around.**

## Sex has consequences!

Cats are extremely fertile animals. A domestic cat can manage up to three litters a year, with an average of four to five kittens apiece. Let's take another arithmetic example. Given that a female can raise as many as fourteen kittens in a year, and assuming they reach the age of a year and they have kittens, and finally, assuming there are always equal numbers of males and females and they all survive, then the progenies of the one cat in only five years would amount to 65,536 children, grandchildren, great-grandchildren, and great-great-grandchildren. A theoretical figure, of course, but one that should make you stop and think. Without a doubt there is nothing more wonderful, more touching, or more fascinating than watching a mother cat raise her young. But do you really know where the little ones are going to be living later on? It goes without saying that simply abandoning them is out of the question. It is also easy to realize that a closed-up house or a one-room apartment likely won't look like new after a bunch of fast-growing young cats has shacked up there for a few weeks. Have you come to the wise decision, based on careful deliberation, not to want to raise a litter of kittens? Then let your cat be neutered or spayed straight away!

The vast majority of house-bound cats get neutered or spayed nowadays. This kind of "mutilation" doesn't mean the same thing to animals as it does to people. Animals won't be indulging in theoretical questions, such as, "Now, how was it when I was still able to . . . ?" For them, getting neutered is merely a relief, since they will be released from futile longings for something they can't have in their living situation. Your cat certainly won't suffer from being neutered, but it will from the chronic frustration of having no outlet for its sex drive.

# UNDERSTANDING AND MISUNDERSTANDING

A cat can express itself in so many different ways. Through sounds, facial expressions, tail signals, and body posture, it lets others of its kind know what mood it's in and what it wants of them. Our yard lions usually articulate clearly and carefully when they "speak" to "their" people. The many eloquent variations of the "meow" are plainly reserved for us humans.

**B**y language, we people usually mean only the spoken word. In a larger sense, however, language encompasses every means of communication with others, including gestures and other body signals and, at least for us, the written word. Cats understand one another through vocalization, as well as through facial expressions and body posture. Apart from the acoustic and visual possibilities of communication, cats also distribute olfactory information. Scent markers, which they leave on special landmarks, function as calling cards or signs, approximating our written language (see also the chapter "At Home and on the Road").

## Oral Language

Cats possess a comprehensive repertoire of vocalizations with which they can make themselves immediately understood. If we divide this vocabulary according to what cats want to express with it, we can distinguish three categories of sounds. In the first category there are "conversational sounds," soft, gentle tones with which a mother cat converses with her young or proffers her invitation to a tom who wants to mate with her. That well-known purring sound also falls into this category. In the second category, cats know how to make calls that range from the soft meow of the lounge leopard to the piercing battle yowl

**A little kitten naturally expresses its own mood through facial expressions and body signals. Through the reactions of other cats, it learns not only an appropriate "colloquial tone," but also to pay close attention to the expressive motions of others and to interpret them correctly.**

135

# UNDERSTANDING AND MISUNDERSTANDING

**ABOVE LEFT: A sound or movement has attracted the attention of this resting cat. Its eyes and ears are trained on the corresponding location.**

**ABOVE RIGHT: While contentedly dozing—a favorite occupation of all cats—the gaze from the cat's half-closed eyes is fixed on emptiness.**

of rivaling tomcats. Finally, in the third category, threatened, frightened, or aggravated cats utter enraged sounds that are understood at once, generally even by noncats. They hiss or "spit" (a short hissing that begins with a hard K sound), and thus sound the obvious warning that a violent attack is in the offing. One cat, preoccupied with something it has just

caught or a larger chunk of particularly choice food, may accost another coming too close with a deep, throaty growl, all the while keeping its teeth clamped around the morsel. This warning sound ("Just as long as it's clear: This is my catch and you stay away from it!") is more reminiscent of a dog than of a cat.

Aside from the mother-child

relationship and sexual or aggressive encounters, cats amongst themselves understand one another predominantly without speech. A good deal of their oral vocabulary, which we know from our own cats, especially the famous meow, seems to be primarily reserved for people. Further discussion of this will come at the end of the chapter.

**You can tell not only by the facial features, but also by the overall body position, what**

**kind of mood the cat is in at the moment. The position of the ears and whiskers, the size of the pupils,**

**or how the tail is held are just as much signals of a cat's mood as hunching its back, crouching, or standing its hairs on end.**

**FROM LEFT TO RIGHT: alert-tense, fearful-aggressive, prepared to attack, peacefully dozing.**

## The Mystery of Purring

Purring belongs to the human notion of a cat as much as its sharp claws do. It isn't known, even nowadays, how cats actually produce this pleasant sound. One prerequisite appears to be that its hyoid bone isn't completely made of bone, as is that of big cats (see also the chapter "Origin and Species"), and something in its body makes the cat vibrate when purring. This much is evident as the vibration can be felt when you touch a purring cat.

Infant kittens can purr even before they can open their eyes. Presumably the original function of purring lies in in-

**ABOVE LEFT**: This little fellow has flattened his ears to the side in a fearful-aggressive manner. The upright posture and narrowed eyes indicate that his desire to attack is greater than his fear.

An unwelcome visitor is fixed with a threatening stare by this tomcat. As he does so, first one then the other ear indignantly turns to the side (BELOW). His face contorted with rage, he attempts to impress his adversary with savage hissing (ABOVE RIGHT). His large, fearful pupils betray his uneasiness.

forming the nursing mother that her young are well. The sound is particularly efficient, since the little ones can utter it while suckling, with their little mouths clamped around the teats. They don't have to interrupt their purring even to swallow.

A cat doesn't purr only as a nursing infant. It keeps on purring right up to the end of its life, and uses the sound to express contentment and well-being. Depending on the social situation, purring can also take on a wider range of meanings. A kitten walks up purring to an adult cat when it wants to invite it to play. A more dominant cat purrs when it approaches a subordinate in a friendly manner, to reassure the other of its harmless intentions. A subordinate, sick, or very weak old cat, on the other hand, purrs as soon as a stronger cat approaches. In this case, purring probably serves to pacify the approaching cat and means something like, "Hey, I'm just weak and harmless, really!"

A mother cat purrs when she joins her young in the nest to calm the little ones. While nursing them, she usually joins in with their contented purring.

You often get the impression that a cat can heighten its own feeling of well-being by purring. Just lying there quietly and being stroked is a treat; being petted and then purring way down in the throat, that's a real treat! Some cats, incidentally, also purr when they're in pain, in fact even when they're at death's door. Might this perhaps constitute a kind of self-comforting autosuggestion? We don't know.

## Facial Expressions

A cat's face is capable of a multitude of expressions and is an unambiguous barometer of mood for mutual communication among cats. Since cats are keen observers, even minute changes in the facial expression of others won't escape them. A person who wants to live together in harmony with a cat will have to get used to paying attention to fine details, such as the size of its pupils, and the position of its ears and long whiskers, to avoid misunderstandings and discrepancies.

In a happy, receptive mood, the facial features of a cat are regular and untroubled, and its ears are pricked. When a feeling of drowsiness descends over the cat, its eyelids gradually close. If something arouses the cat's attention, however, its eyes open wide, its whiskers spread out as far as they can, and its ears are eagerly cocked forward. And yet, everything is still at peace. Should its ears turn to the side and slant backward, its face crease with displeasure, and its lips curl back slightly, this indicates, without a doubt, the advent of fear or annoyance. The anxious cat is readying its defenses while sending its "enemy" a clear warning. Its ears laid flat against its head, pupils dilated, and its face furrowed into a grimace, it hisses, "Not another step. Don't force me to use my claws!"

An angry cat, on the other hand, shows its readiness to attack by slowly lowering its head and facing its adversary. The stare fixed on the latter is steady. (Staring, among cats, is considered a threat.) Its pupils will narrow to tiny slits. The ears are now less flattened, inasmuch as they are turned so that the backs of the ears are toward the adversary. Should the other cat not understand the threat, or not take it seriously, the attack can follow in no time. In contrast with defensive behavior, in an aggressive attack the teeth, not the claws, are utilized.

It is rare that a cat expresses an unadulterated readiness to fight, not accompanied by the least anxiety. After all, it's impossible to tell how strong the adversary really is, and a certain amount of respect can't hurt a seasoned warrior. In general, therefore, elements of an attacking, as well as de-

**LEFT PAGE: Its slightly lowered body position, the way it keeps anxiously looking around, and the uncertain swishing of its tail indicate that this young Siamese feels pretty ill at ease (ABOVE). Thank goodness it's a person I know! With tail held high, it runs over (BELOW), just as it ran to its mother when it was a little kitten.**

**ABOVE RIGHT: Now, just no overly hasty moves! This cat prowling on the hunt is frozen in immobility. Its face and body position bespeak keen alertness.**

**BELOW RIGHT: Even tiny kittens respond to a terrifying adversary by arching their backs in classic cat fashion. Turned broadside, fur on end, they appear to be bigger than they really are. With luck, the adversary will fall for the bluff.**

**This lurking cat crouches without stirring a hair. Only the twitching tail betrays the hunter's excitement.**

**Cats recognize one another by the individual scent of the secretions of glands in their skin. When a cat nuzzles (LEFT), the glands located on the head ensure that the cat's own scent is transmitted to the other. This marking establishes a feeling of belonging together. When two cats meet, they subject each other to a thorough olfactory investigation. This procedure always commences nose to nose (RIGHT).**

fensive, mode are mixed in the facial expressions of an outraged cat. How large the prevalent share of either emotion is in the mood of the moment can best be read from the position of the ears. The more the back of the ear can be seen from the front, the stronger the readiness to attack; in a purely defensive mode, the ears are so folded to the side that only the horizontally held edges of the ears can still be seen from the front.

## Body Language

A cat can unambiguously express its mood or intention not only with its facial expressions, but also with the position of its entire body. Body posture is the more obvious signal visible from a distance, whereas facial expression functions more like fine tuning. In a gradual mood swing, the first thing to change is always the look on the face, in that it reflects even the slightest nuances in mood. Body position generally doesn't change until the emotional state has.

A contented cat often sits on its haunches, it forepaws placed decorously side by side, and its tail coiled around itself. Receptive to all manner of activities, it waits for whatever of interest might come up, or debates what it might undertake.

An uneasy cat, or one that's moody, most often crouches down with its front paws drawn tightly into its chest and its tail curled close to its body. Should another cat, or else an unwelcome person, approach, it can flash out a claw-studded paw from this position. Others of its own species, however, usually recognize the subtle body signals of edginess and then generally respect the desire for distance—it may be, however, that they have obvious preeminence and, along with it, the right of place or way (see the chapter "At Home and on the Road"). In this case, the first cat, now in a downright foul mood, will clear the field and, as a rule, slink off.

### The Arched Back
A dominant adversary that instills terror in a cat will be confronted by the cat's famous arched back. Most cats respond this way to an attacking dog (or even one that's ambling by too close for comfort); stray feral cats also often respond like this to human beings. Kittens frequently arch

## What is the proper way to approach a cat?

Like most animals, cats feel threatened when somebody (or somebody's hand) comes too close too quickly, overstepping a certain tolerable minimum distance. This distance, the so-called critical distance, differs from cat to cat and situation to situation. You first notice you've gone too far when the cat clears out or takes a swipe at your hand. This can even happen with your intimately familiar family cat if your hand takes it by surprise when it has just woken up. This is why you should always address a resting cat before stroking it.

It is no accident that unfamiliar cats slowly move toward each other with caution and always carry out certain rituals to get acquainted. To get to know one another, they sniff each other thoroughly from the tips of their noses to their anuses. Therefore you, a stranger, should give a shy or mistrusting cat the pos-

sibility for a smell-check. Approach it without any sudden moves and hold out your hand to be sniffed. Always wait for the cat to come to you and never try to grab it if it avoids you. This can end in bloody scratches.

A very familiar cat may greet you with a "nose kiss," when it encounters you at eye level. The best thing is to play along with this. You will be displaying not only good intentions, but also good "cat etiquette." Finally, the cat will, with its tail obligingly upright, offer you an anal check. As a human, you don't really have to follow through with this, however—a friendly pat will do the trick! And how do you part ways again after such a detailed cultivation of contact? Whatever you do, you shouldn't shove the cat away. Instead, follow cat etiquette and leave slowly.

**Among adult cats who have developed close social attachments, mutual grooming is perfectly normal. This friendly gesture also helps clean fur inaccessible to its owner's tongue.**

their backs at adult animals unfamiliar to them. The position of the body is always the same: The cat raises the hair along its back and tail, places itself broadside, and hunches its back into an upside-down U. The tail, meanwhile, gets fluffed out from the base and then curved downward like a sickle.

The old German description of a sycophant is of a hunch-backed cat. Actually, the arched cat back does not demonstrate groveling obsequiousness at all, but rather

**Enthusiastically, this domestic tom submits to the affectionate care of the large puma female. Cats really have no difficulty communicating across species frontiers.**

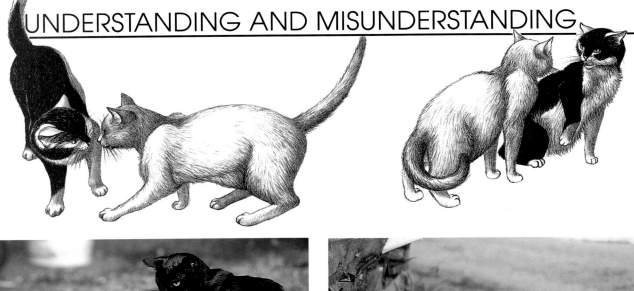

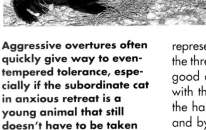

**Aggressive overtures often quickly give way to even-tempered tolerance, especially if the subordinate cat in anxious retreat is a young animal that still doesn't have to be taken seriously (LEFT).**

**Staring at an approaching cat signifies a threat. The appropriate reassuring response is to overtly look away. The unspoken dialogue runs something like this: "Better stay the heck away from me!" "Don't sweat it; I don't want to have anything to do with you anyway" (RIGHT).**

represents the cat's reaction to the threat of attack. There is a good dose of fear mixed in with this reaction. By raising the hair on its back and tail, and by raising the line of its back, a cat can considerably enlarge its silhouette. The purpose of all this is to cut a particularly terrifying figure to intimidate the adversary, so as to clear up the situation, if possible without "losing face" or having to get involved in a fight at all.

In this position, the body expresses the cat's conflicting feelings. On the one hand, it wants to stand its ground and has no intention of leaving; while on the other, its fear of its adversary makes it instinctively shrink back. Thus, the forelegs, closest to the adversary, start to back up, while the hind legs stay where they are. This temporarily compresses the entire cat. When this can't go any farther, the retreating forelegs avoid the back legs by stepping to the side, turning the body sideways. Should the adversary keep coming, the cat finally retreats, although in moving its forelegs first, its hindquarters seem hesitantly to follow suit. This results in a backward, stilt-walking sidestep, always turned broadside toward its enemy, which it doesn't let out of its sight for a moment. If the adversary is intimidated by this "giant cat" with its horrible hissing and in turn retreats, the first cat advances again, stiff-legged, at which time the now "braver" hind legs often over-

**Most encounters between cats that don't know each other proceed in a more or less neutral fashion. Each sniffs at the other and they go their own ways—the subordinate animal in a hurry, the dominant one with deliberate slowness.**

## Encounters of the Feline Kind

Should two cats who don't know each other meet, the first thing they want to find out is whether they can "get a noseful" of and "go on all fours" with each other. Cats take this absolutely literally. They sniff at each other extensively, always starting nose to nose. (Most of the time they don't actually touch noses, however.) Their bodies are slightly lowered, their heads stretched as far forward as possible. It is quite obvious when one distrusts the other. Each animal then tries to sniff the length of the other's body, lastly smelling the other's anal region. But since they are usually both busy keeping their hindquarters away from each other, the two animals end up turning around each other for

a while. If their ears are still receptively pricked forward in curiosity, the encounter will be a friendly one. One of the two cats finally lifts its tail with an obliging gesture and allows the other to smell its backside. Then it's the other's turn. Now they have become acquainted—and usually go their own ways.

Admittedly, this description of a feline encounter is highly idealized. The reality in the majority of cases looks different. In most meetings, the rit-

**Many encounters between cats look so threatening to us that right away we're thinking bloody murder. Yet, the outward show is most often a lot bigger than the underlying intention of attacking.**

take the front half of the body. From time to time, it comes out of its arched stance for brief forays that are always typically defensive in nature, using the claws and not the teeth. All in all, the whole "humpback show" is just an elaborate attempt at bluffing. Should the enemy not be impressed, and in approaching overstep the so-called critical distance, the cat, as a rule, will turn and run away. It then charges off as fast as its legs will carry it.

### The Expressive Tail
Just as the ears are the cat's mood-barometer at its front end, the tail is a barometer at the back end. Held slightly above the ground, the smooth tail indicates the normal state. Fluffed out like a bottle-cleaning brush, it signifies alarm. Horizontally extended from the crouched body, its tip twitching slightly, it is a sign of extreme concentration and excitement. The cat may be just

lying in wait for a prey animal or watching a dog in the distance, or it may have sighted an unwelcome fellow cat. If the tail now starts swishing back and forth excitedly, the cat is definitely about to make its move. A vertically raised tail always signals a markedly friendly mood. Kittens respond this way to the approach of their mother. Feline friends who live with one another in a group greet each other this way, if only in passing.

When a cat lives with humans, it often shares its home with other pets. In daily life, each becomes acquainted with the other pet (or pets) and knows how to adapt. While there are always some misunderstandings between dogs and cats, as the same gestures in their respective "languages" have different meanings, both animals are, of course, able to learn. Especially when a puppy and a kitten grow up together, there are really very few difficulties. Each speedily learns the "foreign language" of the other.

ual breaks down right after the initial nose-to-nose sniffing. For no sooner does one cat attempt to take the next step in getting closer by smelling the other's neck than it has demonstrated a greater self-confidence. This leaves the other one, which for its part was not so "brave," to take a more or less defensive stance. It cowers and slinks away, its ears now flattened. If the first cat persists in its approach of the second, the latter's defense is made more evident by hissing or a cuff of the paw. In the end, the subordinate cat slinks off and then comes to a standstill some distance away, turning around to face the other cat. This one, meanwhile, has given the spot where its uncertain adversary had been standing or sitting before a good going over with its nose. Most often, it now slowly wanders after the one that ran away, to continue its efforts at smelling it out close up. It will have no better luck than the first time and, in fact, will likely run into stronger de-

**With its high degree of social intelligence, there is no doubt a cat can learn to accept certain little animals as family members; however, a cat that is not allowed to pounce on potential prey will get stressed out and frustrated in the long run.**

fenses. The whole game can repeat itself several times. It really depends on the temperament and mood of the dominant cat whether it finally gives up any further attempts to seek contact, or whether, in the end, grown irritable and aggressive, it makes a cut-and-dried attack.

## Understanding Across Species Frontiers

Cats generally have no difficulty communicating amongst themselves. This is true not only for domestic cats, but also for the entire extended family of wild cats. The ways of behaving and the gestures of the various species of felids—big cats as well as small cats—are alike

Since cats pay attention to the finest nuances in facial expression and body position in order to understand one another, we people must seem incredibly dense to them. Thus, they usually use deliberately clear "language" when addressing us. Their vocabulary frequently stems from the mother-child relationship. Just like a kitten with its mother, a family cat will beg "its" people for food.

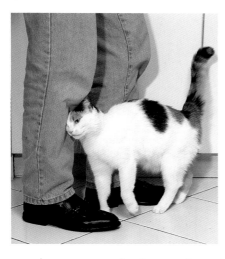  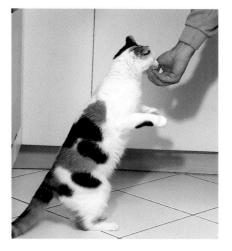

to such a great extent that there are hardly any misunderstandings across the lines of the species.

## Misunderstandings between Cats and Dogs

It is different between cats and dogs. It's true that there is no question of a "primal hostility," as plenty of cats and dogs get along fine. But even animals that are well-disposed toward one another can completely misunderstand each other from time to time. This happens when similar innate gestures and ways of behaving carry a different significance for the respective species. An absolutely classic example of this is the raising of a forepaw. For a dog, this is an invitation to play; for a cat, it's a final warning before it starts hauling out with its claws. It's no wonder that so many inexpe-

rienced dogs are walking around with bloody scratches on their noses. It is well known that dogs wag their tails to express joy and affection. When a cat's tail swishes madly back and forth, this means excitement and utter displeasure. Consequently, a cat may assume that the waggy-tailed dog is about to do something to harm it, while a dog might suppose the waggy-tailed cat is happy to see it. When a cat feels threatened at close quarters, it throws itself on the ground to be able to defend itself with all its claws in unison. For a dog, this lying-on-your-back is a gesture of humility, by which a subordinate fighter indicates capitulation to the dominant party. If a cat throws itself on its back in front of a dog, the latter must find it pretty unfair and against all the rules of the game when, upon its peaceful approach, it is at-

tacked by claws. The dog really can't be blamed for responding pretty sourly.

However, cats as well as dogs can learn how to deal properly with the idiosyncrasies of the other and understand the other's language—and then become good buddies.

## Communication between Cats and People

We people are in the habit of using our word-language to communicate with one another. With the greatest casualness we transfer this to animals that live with us. Surveys undertaken in the course of socio-biological studies have shown that over 95 percent of all cat owners regularly talk to their animals. Now, it's true cats don't understand everything, but they do understand a lot. While they won't exactly catch on to a discourse on pol-

itics or science, they do know well enough the meaning of a lot of words and phrases in everyday speech.

And because cats are much better observers than we are, they also take in the slightest changes in body posture and the finest nuances in the gestures of "their" people. This means they can not only assess the person's mood with great accuracy, but they can also often "foresee" an intention to do something—betrayed by a stiffening of the back or an unconscious glance in a particular direction—even before a word has been spoken or the particular person has gotten up out of a chair.

Conversely, a cat that wants to make itself understood by people has to make itself pretty darn clear. Compared with the behavior of cats amongst themselves, the gestures of request and affection directed at

# UNDERSTANDING AND MISUNDERSTANDING

people are oftentimes extremely exaggerated or are repeated several times. You definitely get the impression that manycats think people are incredibly dense. They act no differently than we do when we speak extremely slowly and deliberately to somebody who doesn't quite get the point.

## The Meow Dictionary

When a cat meows, it wants its people to pay attention to it. It can be motivated by a wide variety of reasons, and the corresponding meows sound very different.

Many cats utter a characteristic greeting sound on returning from an extended tour outside or when you encounter them unexpectedly somewhere in the house. This "Hello!" in cat language may sound like "Meh!" or "Eh!" It's a very brief sound uttered through almost closed lips. You often hear the same greeting from behind when you are busy doing something (for instance, sitting at your desk writing a cat book), but the cat thinks it's time for you to preoccupy yourself with it instead.

Far more insistent is the sound of the request to refill the empty food dish—at long last. With most cats there is a direct correlation: The emptier the stomach, the more emphatic and louder the meow.

There are, however, also feline actors who, after meowing for some time, come up with a practiced poor-hungry-little-kitty look and then, with a heartrending silent "Meooow," break down every human resistance.

## Why does a cat sometimes scratch when its belly is being stroked?

If your lounge leopard throws itself sprawling on the floor in front of your feet and stretches out with its belly toward you, this is a great show of friendship and trust. It would like to have its belly stroked, just the way its mother massaged its stomach with her tongue when it was an infant. You really should comply with this request. Be careful, though, especially with toms. It is in an adult cat's repertoire of fighting behavior to throw itself on its back and "work over" its adversary with all fours in a close physical fight. With some cats, this defensive behavior suddenly surfaces when their stomachs are touched. Out of the blue, the cat will kick and lash out at the petting hand, with its claws at least somewhat extended. Please don't blame the cat. It doesn't mean to be nasty; it's just an arbitrary, reflexive response. Many cats that live with people have learned to suppress this reflex because they adore being petted; others, at the very least, still twitch their hind legs. The legs of cats experienced in fighting, usually tomcats, do tend to develop a life of their own and "fight." If only you could see the embarrassed look on my tomcat's face as he pulls away when this happens during an otherwise enjoyable session of stomach caressing!

pending on its character, one cat squawks before it has even been grazed, and another only when it has actually been hurt. And it depends on the extent of its distress whether this screech is an annoyed "Just watch your step!" or an anxious "He-e-e-lp!"

**What a great treat to be fondled and stroked like that! Obviously the cat is transported back to kitten-dom and reminded of its mother giving it a soothing lick and working its fur with her tongue. Even the biggest cat will purr when being stroked like a little kitten in the nest.**

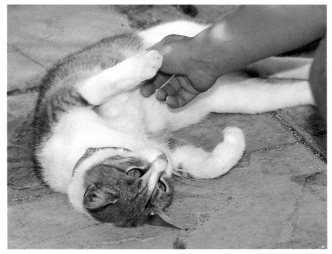

Another variation of the meow means "Let me out!" or "Let me in!" whichever the case might be. Depending on the character of the cat or the mood of the day, this vocalization can have the overtones of an absolute imperative or of a plaintive lament.

And then there's the shrill "Ow!" leaving the "Me" off, usually uttered when an inattentive person is just about to sit down on the chair in which the cat is curled up sleeping, or when the person unintentionally steps backward on the cat's paw or tail. In turn, de-

**People who catch a resting cat unawares by their approach, even if it is with well-meaning petting, may provoke an instinctive defensiveness on the part of the startled cat that can be truly painful to the hand.**

# AT HOME AND ON THE ROAD

One cat controls a territory of many acres, another is satisfied with the floor space of a small apartment. The one lives as a loner, the other as a member of a social feline group. Many develop close relationships with a single person, whom they consider to be the "super cat." In science there is now talk of the "endless social diversity" of cats.

**U**ntil recently very little was known about the life of the domestic free-ranging cat. Cats' pronounced talents for eluding pursuit or observation on soft yet sturdy paws made systematic studies in the open country well-nigh impossible. For some fifteen years, however, behaviorists have used biotelemetry—a collar with a tiny transmitter provides information about the whereabouts of a cat—and through such radio-tracking much new knowledge has been gained about free-ranging cats.

## The Home

The cat's actual home is called the first-order home or primary home. It is most often a house (or even only a room), a barn for farm cats, a warehouse shed or ruin for feral street cats. This is where the cat sleeps, where the young grow up, where it comes when it is sick or hurt and needs quiet. The immediate surroundings of this home it knows inside and out. It is familiar with every corner, every cranny to slip through and every way to climb up. Certain preferred spots are used as places to sunbathe, as lookouts, or as places to catch forty winks in between times. In biological terminology, these areas are called second-order homes or secondary homes. Lengthy travel, however, regularly leads cats far beyond the boundaries of their home ranges.

## Home Ranges and Cat Trails

Out in the open country, cats usually roam in regions of between 125 and 250 acres (fifty and one hundred hectares) in area. By comparison, the majority of feline territories within townships and metropolitan areas are obviously smaller. In the suburbs of London, for instance, ranges for solitary cats of less than a quarter of an

**En route in open terrain, a cat is constantly busy scrutinizing the scent markings left by other cats. Scent markings, by and large, have the function of a daily paper and provide the roaming cat with up-to-date information about who was where when, and whether, for instance, an unfamiliar cat went by.**

# AT HOME AND ON THE ROAD

Cats do not just stay in the immediate vicinity of their homes, but regularly go on extensive patrols through the surrounding areas. Over the last few years, behaviorists have repeatedly made the effort to pursue various cats day and night on their excursions. It turns out that in rural areas cats frequent a range of up to 0.4 square miles (one square kilometer). For powerful toms, especially during the mating season, the personal range can even be about a factorial larger.

When the paths taken by cats were marked out on thumbnail maps, it became evident that they do not wander around all over the place but generally stick to regular trails. Over hill and dale, roofs and stairways, cats trot by. They never seem aimless when they are on the move, but always look as though they have a clear idea of where they want to go.

acre (0.1 hectare) have been measured. Under somewhat natural conditions, the home ranges of males are always larger than the home ranges of females, three and one-half times larger on the average.

Within its range, a cat has specific hunting, fighting, courtship, and mating places that it visits more or less regularly, and all of these places are both interconnected and individually connected to the home by a close-knit network of trails. When cats' movements started to be carefully recorded, it was noted that they actually use fixed paths in their territory. The inhabitants of the territory practically never set foot on the expanses between these paths. In a wintry, snow-covered yard, it is easy to see that the tracks rarely cross open

spaces. Cats on the move prefer the cover of hedges, fences, or other landmarks, even if these are often circuitous routes. A cat takes a short, direct route with no guaranteed flanking cover only when it is in a definite hurry or when it is moving on home turf where it feels absolutely safe.

## Perfumed Calling Card

Cats always take great pains to leave their personal calling cards in the form of scent markings at clearly defined points along their routes. Later, another cat on a stroll through the neighborhood will be able to "read" from the scent marking who was there, and when.

Males especially, but certainly females as well, have the habit of spraying urine in a fine stream on vertical landmarks such as trees, bushes, posts, or walls, and also indoors on doorjambs and on furniture. Cats often rub their heads on the now-fragrant objects and then rub up against

other objects in other locations. Cats usually rub their heads, flanks, or rear ends on a few objects along their way as a matter of routine. As they have distinctive scent glands in those particular areas of the body, when they rub up against things, they are distributing their own individual perfumes in their surroundings. They also have scent glands on the pads of their toes, and these secretions are transferred when cats sharpen their claws on the base of trees or on fence slats.

**Cats love high-lying lookouts. Up there, no enemy can easily approach undetected. At the same time, the whole region is in sight and one can take in what's happening on the cat scene. "Seeing and being seen," is the motto of cats patrolling their territory.**

## Can having a cat without outdoor access be justified?

This question is a highly controversial one among cat owners, breeders, and veterinarians alike. Where a cat can roam, hunt, and encounter other cats—in yards, green spaces, or even in meadows and fields—I personally plead for letting it run. The hunting instinct, as well as the territorial and social behavior of cats, is simply tailored to life in a spacious area. If your dwelling permits, you should facilitate a fitting feline lifestyle by allowing regular access outdoors. There is no doubt, however, of the many dangers lurking for cats in our "civilized" environment. First and foremost, there is motorized traffic. Then, there are rat poison, herbicides, dogs trained to hunt cats, and animal catchers engaged in the dubious trade of animals for research, all of which can become the undoing of free-ranging cats. And yet, my cats (to which I'm terribly attached) may go in and out whenever the mood takes them.

If you are afraid of your cat being stolen by animal-catchers, have the veterinarian tattoo a registered number inside its ear. Presently, there is a trend toward inserting a unique microchip under the cat's skin, and the cat is then registered in a computer network. Registered cats are uninteresting as merchandise since they won't, as a rule, be bought by research laboratories. Also, vaccinations against infectious diseases are extremely important for free-ranging cats, as are regular check-ups for parasite infestations.

If you can't or won't let your cat go outside, then you must ensure an interior arrangement that befits a cat and has adequate stimulus for physical activity. A cat that has been kept indoors from birth won't be missing much really. Still, if your parlor panther has no way to live out its needs, neither you nor it will be very happy: Behavioral disorders are practically guaranteed in a frustrated cat. And, a cat that has become accustomed to a lifestyle with plenty of freedom to move won't, as a rule, let you turn it into an indoor house cat.

---

Whereas depositing and leaving feces behind is a personal "scent threat," which is typical of dominating toms (see the chapter "Cleanliness and Grooming"), perfuming landmarks by spraying, rubbing, or scratching obviously doesn't exert any intimidating effect at all. A cat sniffing another's marking doesn't then retreat. Usually, after it has calmly taken time to smell it extensively, it goes on its way. Oftentimes, it quickly sprays or rubs its own perfume over the stranger's before it moves on.

Most probably, scent markings among cats act like memos about who went where when. The "scent news" enables a cat to gauge how far away the predecessor already

**A cat can probably tell by scent traces, which it sniffs meticulously, not only that another cat has been there but probably even which of the cats it is acquainted with passed by.**

is. Thus it can avoid an unwanted encounter. Each personal scent substance begins to lose the intensity of its fragrance as soon as it is deposited. This is because it decomposes chemically when it comes into contact with the oxygen in the air. Because the scent markings gradually weaken and change, a cat can estimate the time that has passed since the marking was placed. Every cat is concerned about undertaking regular patrols through its territory to keep its own scent markings fresh.

## Traffic Control in Cat Territory

As a rule, ranges of neighboring cats overlap over wide areas. This means that normally the trail network, as well as the preferred hunting terrain, is shared by several cats. Shared use doesn't, however, also mean simultaneous use. Cats know how to avoid personal encounters with other cats. Even cats that share a primary home mostly make solitary patrols through the surrounding area.

When two cats in the open countryside see each other in good time and can watch each

**ABOVE LEFT: By spraying urine to which an extremely penetrating odorous secretion from the anal glands is added, tomcats mark points in the landscape that appear strategically significant to them with their own personal scent.**

**ABOVE RIGHT: Scratching doesn't just sharpen the claws, it marks territory as well. Besides the obviously visible scratches, the secretion from scent glands located in the pads of the toes are left behind on the base of the object.**

**BELOW: On walks through their territories, cats are always preoccupied with leaving behind their personal calling cards in the form of scent markings on noticeable spots. To do this, they often rub their cheeks against hard objects. This results in a more discreet** memo than spraying urine, and this fleeting message has to be refreshed more frequently. Through careful smelling, the cat checks to see whether the fragrance of the marked spot corresponds to its sense of what it should be, or whether more rubbing is necessary.

## In or out – can't cats ever make up their minds?

Surely all cat owners have sighed this when they let their house mate out the door at its request, only to let it back in five minutes later through a window—once again in response to insistent meowing. No sooner are they inside than they often immediately want to go back out again. This can be nerve-racking. Cats must certainly find doors one of the most unpleasant of human inventions. Doors constantly get in the way of the range patrols they undertake to pick up the latest information about the activities of their colleagues from around the neighborhood.

Should you have the opportunity, do your cat (and yourself) the favor of putting in a special cat door so it can slip in and out as it pleases. Such cat-flaps, which swing freely to both sides, can be built into the front door, basement door, or even into a window. They can be purchased cheaply at any pet supply store—if you don't want to tinker and make one yourself. An opening with an inside measurement of seven by seven inches (eighteen by eighteen centimeters) is plenty for a cat to slip through comfortably.

good time and can watch each other, they very rarely come to blows. They sit down and after some time both retreat, or one takes the initiative and the other waits until the first one has crossed an intersection. Most cats prefer to go out of their way to avoid conflict or come to an arrangement through eye contact. Situations where the animals run across one another by surprise in unseen places are, on the other hand, rife with possibilities for conflict. Most often what happens is an exchange of threatening gestures and hissing, which, from time to time, can also develop into a violent altercation. When the right of way, and therefore personal prestige, is at issue, female cats, it might be mentioned, have proven themselves to be much more bloodthirsty and intolerant than males.

The outcome of quarrels or

**A cat unexpectedly popping up in the immediate vicinity puts its fellow in a tight spot. A conflict is often the inevitable outcome of such an unplanned meeting.**

An encounter between two cats always proceeds differently, depending not only on which two animals meet up, but also on what moods they happen to be in. Usually cats from a small range know one another personally and are very well informed about the rank of each of the others. Cats don't jump all over each other at the drop of a hat. Through eye contact and finely nuanced body signals each can let the others know its mood and state of mind from a distance. Even animals that should actually be on bad terms, according to the rules of feline society, frequently manage to avoid a fight and still "save face" through proper comportment. One, for instance, looks away long enough so that the other has the opportunity to get out of reach at a measured pace. If it comes to a face-to-face encounter (ABOVE LEFT; BELOW LEFT), one of the animals usually takes the initiative and "greets" the other, extending its nose (ABOVE RIGHT). While mutually sniffing (BELOW RIGHT), both cats want to establish whether they can "get a noseful" of the other.

quite serious fights over territorial rights establishes the future ranking order between the two adversarial parties. Dominance, once gained, counts only for the locale of the confrontation. In another spot in the territory, a fight between the same animals can easily turn out the other way around. (In general, confidence, and along with it the courage to fight, certainly increase the closer the cat is to its primary home.) Even the time at which the decisive encounter takes place plays a role. In feline traffic flow, there are such complicated rules as, for instance, in the mornings tomcat A has priority on a certain garden wall and, conversely, in the afternoons tomcat B does.

All of this applies primarily to the more-or-less neutral terrain of the home range, or secondary home. The primary home, especially the core and its immediate environs, is usually adamantly defended against interlopers. Once again, females generally respond much more angrily than toms. Yet, along with this, there is usually some individual access permitted to particular animals, no matter whether they are dominant or subordinate. People can certainly recognize themselves in this behavior.

## Cats – Gregarious Loners

Many cats in the wild are, without a doubt, typical loners. Except for mating season and while raising young, they roam around alone and through appropriate scratching and rubbing behavior make sure that no other cats crowd them too much. Although the domestic cat resembles its wild cousins in many ways, on one point it has fundamentally changed in the course of its domestication: It has evolved a capacity for social attachments. Many cats really value the company of others of their kind. They don't

consider people merely as two-legged food-donors, either, but as social partners with whom they can, and often do, build distinctly close relationships.

## The Important Phase of Socialization

There is a sensitive period or sensitive phase in kittendom that is crucial for molding later social or asocial behavior. This particular period of interaction

**The face of this old campaigner is marked by the numerous fights he has fought over the course of his lifetime.**

with other living beings—be they other cats, other animals, or even people—has a more lasting effect than any other period in life. For cats, the sensitive phase of socialization lies between the second and seventh week of life. This means kittens that have intensive and pleasant human contact, as a rule, develop into family cats that are friendly to people, whereas cats that have

grown up wild will probably remain timid and reserved all their lives.

Cats fearful of human contact are not necessarily asocial with other cats. If they are raised in a social group of cats, they usually get along excellently with other cats later on in life. Intraspecies and extraspecies socialization are obviously quite independent of one another in

the development of a cat's personality.

### The Lap Cat: an Overgrown Child

If you compare cats living in close relationships with people with wild or free-ranging domestic cats, one thing becomes very clear: Family lap cats exhibit a whole array of behavior that occurs only during kittendom in feral cats. A shelf full of cans of cat food, lined up like kitchen ware, relieves it of the necessity of ever having to truly grow up and deal with the serious side of life (in two words: acquiring food). The people tending it are seen not only as dominant "super cats," but also as mother figures. Fellow cats that live in the same household assume the role of littermates. They play with one another, often sleep closely snuggled together, and beg their human "mother," with upright tails and insistent rubbing, for food. Sitting in a person's lap while being stroked, a cat must surely feel the same sense of well-being it felt way back when its real mother groomed, warmed, and nursed it in the security of the nest. It now treads and kneads the soft human lap with its forepaws

**Before an encounter reaches the level of a serious fight, the adversaries most often spend some time circling each other. They mutually threaten and size each other up. As a sign of great self-assurance, the tail is spread away from the body and curved in a sickle-shape and pointed stiffly to the ground. If neither gives way, the fight is fought out tooth and claw (drawing).**

**This young Abyssinian cat is not at all on good terms with the other cat. She just recently joined a group of cats and is now attempting to gain respect so she can hold her own in her new home. She exhibits typical defensive behavior: Her face is contorted into an aggressive grimace; her body is fearfully crouched down. As the distance to the "enemy" is less than the just barely acceptable minimum, the little cat acts according to the long-standing principle: Offense is the best defense. Quite obviously she isn't really being taken seriously yet by her adversary, otherwise the latter's reaction would certainly be more marked.**

**In contrast with most cats in the wild—which lead a solitary life, except during the mating season—over the thousands of years of their domestication, domestic cats have developed the capacity for social attachments. Many truly value the company of other familiar cats. Even as adults, they often seek out intimate physical contact with fellow felines when they want to sleep, just as they used to do as infants in the nest with their littermates. Wherever there is a daily food ration for all, as on many farms, there is no call for rivalry. The animals in the group know one another and eat close together as a matter of course. Still, woe to the cat that is a stranger to the group should it dare to interfere!**

just as it massaged its mother's stomach as an infant kitten to stimulate the flow of milk.

### Cat Hang-Outs

Today we know a lot about cats and their way of life, and yet there are still behavior patterns for which we really can't see any rhyme or reason. One of these is the rarely observed occasion when cats hang out together. Rarely observed because they gather at night, and in contrast with aggressive feline encounters, which are deafening, hanging out proceeds calmly and quietly. The neighborhood cats, mostly toms, but also emancipated feline females, casually get together at a peaceful, safe, and centrally located place. They meet, sit or lie around, relax, and maybe engage in some mutual grooming. Only rarely is a brief hiss to be heard, when one inadvertently crowds another. After some time, the

circle finally breaks up again and they all go home. Do cats hang out like this for pretty much the same reason many people stop in at the tavern in the evening to "grab a quick beer"?

### Social Hierarchies

In a group of local cats, one cat rarely enjoys complete dominance. As a rule, individual encounters establish who has to concede which privileges to whom. Whatever issues still need clarification are fought out in extensive ritualized fights according to the current contest rules.

The ranking order among female cats usually isn't very strict and is primarily based on their roles as mothers. With each litter, and especially when she is carrying young, the status of a female cat rises tremendously. If she is spayed after several litters, her rank takes a nose-dive. Females that get

spayed before they have ever had young have no chance of ever holding high rank.

The hierarchy of tomcats is based on entirely different laws. Here the concern is bravado and fighting power. The local unneutered toms form a kind of dueling bond or brotherhood. A newcomer, or a young male just come into his prime, first has to gain his place through a series of fights. If he withstands this "baptism by fire," he is accepted into the fraternity. Henceforth, he has to fight only when he himself challenges a tom of superior rank or when he is challenged by one of subordinate rank. These contests for rank within the fraternity proceed with a lot of racket, it's true, but for the most part they are ritualized fights not intended to knock the adversary out of the running altogether. The toms purposefully target well-padded parts of the body and

## What should you do when there's a cat fight?

It is best not to interfere. For one thing, it generally all looks a lot worse (and sounds a lot worse) than in fact it is. Most cats make an ungodly show of a confrontation. For another, you risk getting badly scratched when you intervene with bare hands (human skin is thinner than feline fur—remember that!). And then, every cat has to fight itself into a position in feline society if it wants be a regular part of this society. Should you disengage the fight this once, it will be made up for at the next opportunity. Cats of both sexes just happen to insist on relationships being clearly established.

Should you believe you really do have to step in because a subordinate cat is having its hide whipped, the best method is to use a water pistol with a powerful, long-range jet. A well-aimed shot can irritate the dominant cat just long enough to allow the subordinate an opportunity to beat a retreat.

those protected by thick fur. A slashed ear or other injury represents an accidental consequence of the duel rather than an intentional one. (Fights outside one's own fraternity are another matter. Here, really damaging fights are frequently undertaken, with no thought of avoiding injury, and often they result in serious wounds.) If a tomcat that has already fought for a certain rank is neutered, he inevitably slips down the social ladder. Castration before the age of sexual maturity excludes the tomcat from the neighborhood fraternity from the outset.

No matter how social they may be, cats do need a certain amount of elbow room. Behaviorists think a cat must be able to keep a distance of at least twenty inches (fifty centimeters) from other cats. If cats are kept at close quarters, the frequency of scrapping and serious fighting increases dramatically, and soon an entirely different type of social structure develops. One or two "rulers" will hold sway over a more or less equally ranked middle class and one or

**Female cats can develop social attachments to the extent that they even raise their young communally. These cat friends not only share the same nest or nesting site, but also communally suckle the little ones, or one mother will warm and tend all the young until the other has rested or has returned from a hunting excursion.**

more completely suppressed outsiders.

## Population Density

Among cats in the wild, as among feral domestic cats, it depends on the amount of available food how many animals live in a particular area. In the wild, one to five cats will live in an area of 250 acres (one hundred hectares), depending on the lay of the land and the abundance of prey. Where their diet is enriched by "subsidies" from people, for instance on farms, the population density of cats can reach as many as fifty animals per 250 acres (one hundred hectares). Close to profitable food sources, such as garbage dumps, fishing harbors, or major city squares where "fools for cats" daily distribute provender by the bucketful, the cat population can rise to two thousand animals per 250

acres (one hundred hectares). In a Japanese fishing village, 2,350 cats were counted in a region of this size—all strays, would you believe!

## Feral Street Clans

The greater the density of the cat population, the more likely cats are to live in social groups rather than alone. In the feral cat population of major cities or harbors, the animals don't merely mutually tolerate one another; one can often observe active social behavior. Whether in New York, Vancouver, London, or another major city, street cats form clans and strike off together

through their not-exactly-easy feline life. On average, fifteen to twenty adult cats occupy a particular quarter in the city and together defend it against intruders. An alpha-male stands at the head of the bunch. His main duty is to safeguard the territory against cats that don't belong to the clan. This he does through scent markings and, if necessary, through claw control. He by no means plays first fiddle with the females in his clan, who mate with various toms (including subordinates) to reduce the danger of a tom treacherously attacking their young. After all, he would have to fear that they were his own

(see the chapter "Birth and Raising"). For their part, the tomcats in a clan don't fight over females in heat. But then, it wouldn't make much sense to do so, since with such a density of toms in the area there would always be a third one laughing on the sidelines ready to step in for both the dueling parties. The females in a clan frequently raise their young communally. This begins with mutual midwife service at the birth and extends to reciprocal nursing of the young and the institution of a day-nursery, in which the little ones are under the supervision of several wetnurses or aunts while their mothers are grooming themselves or off hunting.

It would surely be no exaggeration to call this an out-

and-out behavioral revolution. The basis for this miraculous transformation of cats from solitary creatures to communal creatures is still a mystery to behaviorists. Did cats simply learn that it's easier to survive in a group than alone, or did the inherited characteristics in recent times change so drastically? Or have cats actually been leading active group lives in the asphalt jungle of cities for a long time already without anybody noticing until now?

It is not only cats that live together in a human household that have active social lives. In regions with higher cat population densities, "wild" street cats also join together in groups. For cats, however, living in a group doesn't mean they are all together all the time. Each cat goes on its daily territorial surveys and hunting excursions alone. The separate ranges overlap extensively, though, and the animals know and tolerate one another. In the core of the home range, in the cat's actual home, they often take up communal shelter and share equally amongst themselves an abundant, regular source of free food. Various long-term studies have shown that the composition of such feline associations is surprisingly stable. Most animals, especially the females, have a lifetime membership in the group into which they were born. The group gladly spends leisure hours together: The members wash themselves, rest lying close to one another, sometimes even mutually groom each other's fur.

Cats include the rooftops of human settlements in their territory, as a second floor, so to speak. Here, a mother cat is just leading her half-grown young out for a walk; at other times, the house roof serves as a meeting place for a number of cats.

# OLD AGE & ILLNESS

A cat's life isn't all sunshine and frolic. Parasites, viral infections, and traumatic experiences make cats physically and mentally ill. And as cats advance in years, minor complaints often turn into serious physical ailments that make the final years those of illness and decrepitude.

## Parasites

With the hygienic way of life we lead today, parasites frequently arouse more worry and fear than actual illness. We consider illness a misfortune that occurs through no fault of our own; lice, fleas, and parasites, on the other hand, are seen as signs of filth and neglect and carry with them a sense of shame. Humans transfer this attitude to animals living in their care. Even if the human loathing of parasites seems somewhat excessive, an attempt to control uninvited parasitic guests is quite sensible. Parasites are not intent on killing off their hosts straight away (they would

At the best of times a cat's life is often fraught with danger. Whereas predators and hunters used to be the traditional enemies of wildcats, today's domestic cats are confronted by a variety of technological and chemical contaminants produced by an increasingly unnatural environment. To survive and grow old with dignity is a profound challenge to the feline. In addition to the injuries cats suffer in fights with each other and with other animals or from accidents, they can also be afflicted by a whole battery of illnesses. Fortunate indeed is the cat that is in the care of a human family that provides access to the services of a veterinarian! A feral cat, however, will just have to see where it ends up—which all too often is by the wayside. Animal parasites that live in or on cats are a relatively minor problem.

then be, as it were, cutting off the branch on which they sit), but they are not exactly beneficial to the well-being of their hosts either. If an animal is already weakened, a few parasites can lead to a massive parasitic infestation that, sooner or later, will do the host in. Cats that have free access to the outdoors will, even with the best of care, keep "catching" troublesome lodgers. Like practically all wild animals, feral cats carry a varied assortment of parasites as a matter of course. Parasites are categorized according to their position on or within the body of the host animal, or, in technical terms, as endo- or ecto-parasites. In the following discussion, I will mention only a few of the parasites that frequently plague cats.

## Roundworms

One of the most common parasites that lives in and off cats is the roundworm (*Ascaris*), which affects mainly young cats. The adult spiral-shaped worms are two and one-half to four inches (six to ten centimeters) long and live on the contents of the intestines. In a major infestation, they extract a considerable portion of their host's food, so that a cat can eat constantly and still loose weight until it's no more than skin and bones. Before it arrives in the cat's intestine, the roundworm will have traveled a long road. Roundworm eggs are microscopically small and can stay alive for months inert

**Being sick, or having a fever or pains, is a worrisome situation for a cat. Naturally, it doesn't understand what is going on. Instinctively it seeks out a warm spot and lies there quietly.**

Parasites are tiny organisms that are omnipresent in nature and against which no animal is safeguarded. Severe infestations can seriously impair the health of the host animal. For the well-tended house cat, therefore, preventive steps and combative measures are strongly recommended. If your cat is scratching itself frequently and frenetically and then, on closer inspection of its fur, you find tiny black "dots" climbing around among the hairs (ABOVE LEFT), it is high time for a de-fleaing campaign with flea powder (ABOVE RIGHT).

Brown-black crumbs and sticky clumps in the ears (BELOW LEFT) are a sign that the cat has ear mites. These mites (which, incidentally, cannot be transmitted to humans) are barely visible to the naked eye but are very itchy for the cat.

Tapeworms that live in the intestines of cats and commandeer their share of digested food pulp produce body segments containing eggs that are eliminated from time to time via the anus (BELOW RIGHT).

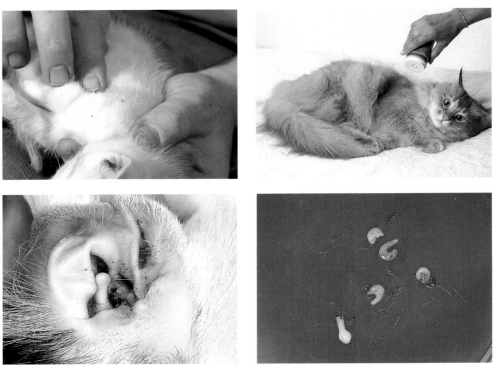

in the ground. They are carried with dust by the wind and tracked into houses on the soles of shoes. If the eggs are picked up by a cat, larvae hatch and work their way through the stomach walls, reaching the lungs by way of the bloodstream or lymph vessels. From the lungs, they continue their way through the windpipe into the pharynx. The cat will then inadvertently swallow the minute larvae, which this time end up in the stomach and intestinal tract for good.

### Tapeworms

These segmented worms—which vary in length from eight to over twenty-four inches (twenty to over sixty centimeters), depending on the variety—embed themselves into the cat's intestinal wall by means of a circle of hooks and suckers they have on their heads. As a tapeworm is surrounded in its habitat by food pulp that has already been broken down by the cat's digestive juices, it can do without an intestine of its own. Tapeworms absorb food through the complete surface area of their bodies. Now and then, they excrete single body segments bursting with eggs from their hind sections. The cat eliminates these whitish tapeworm segments through its anus. The eggs now have to be picked up by a specific species of "intermediate host," in which they develop into so-called bladder worms (Cysticerci). At this stage, they can resettle into the cat if it eats the intermediate host. Such intermediate hosts can be fleas the cat licks up and swallows while grooming its fur, but also mice and rats. Industrious mousers can hardly avoid ingesting tapeworms along with their tasty prey.

### Fleas

These nimble jumpers are real pests. With its proboscis, a flea pierces the cat's skin and feeds by sucking up the cat's blood. The saliva the flea injects into the tiny wound contains an anticoagulant so that a blood clot won't develop as quickly and block the spot where the flea is sucking. This saliva makes the bite itch terribly, causing the cat to scratch itself madly. This, in turn, can lead to large inflamed patches of skin. In addition to cat fleas (*Ctenocephalides felis*), occasionally dog fleas (*Ctenocephalides canis*) get into a cat's fur. Fleas usually stay on the host animal to feed from one to three hours per day. In between times, they hop off and wait on the ground or floor for the appearance of another unsuspecting host. Female fleas lay their eggs in cracks and corners on the ground, or directly onto the cat's fur. The larvae that then hatch feed on mold and organic waste or on the excrement of adult fleas, which consists of incompletely digested blood. Finally the larvae pupate and, after an immobile pupa stage lasting a few days or (in the winter) several months, a new generation of fleas emerge that jump on the first cat that comes along.

**Hardly any cat is thrilled about a visit to the veterinarian, no matter how friendly the assistant is as she fondles it. As part of the physical examination, the veterinarian carefully feels and probes the abdominal organs of the cat.**

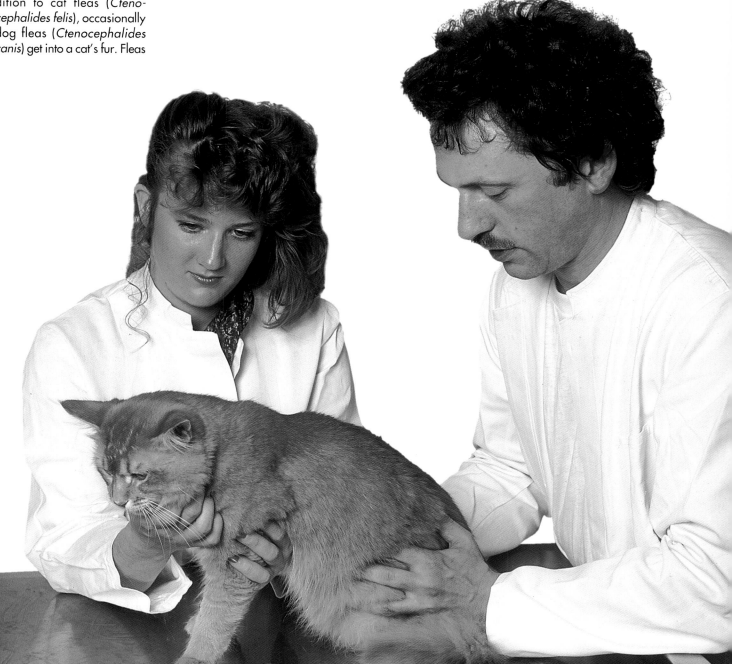

## Common Infectious Diseases

Cats are tough animals that can survive even severe injuries surprisingly well; however, they have much less resistance to viral infections. Feline distemper, rhinotracheitis, and rabies are true cat killers, which today, thanks to modern vaccines for our house cats, have lost much of their horror. Since this is not a book on veterinary medicine, only two of the manifold number of feline infectious diseases will be discussed in brief.

Feline distemper (not related to canine distemper), probably the worst of cat diseases, has had many names—cat plague, cat scourge, feline enteritis—and is known in pro-

**A little kitten sick with an acute case of rhinotracheitis is really a heart-rending sight.**

fessional jargon as panleukopenia or enteritis infectiosa. It is an inflammation of the pharynx and digestive tract. The cause, a highly infectious virus, is to be found in all the eliminations of a sick cat. Once spread in the vicinity, this virus can remain infectious for months. Cats can pick up the

virus almost anywhere. Kittens up until they are about two years of age are particularly susceptible. Unborn kittens can even be infected inside the womb. Without veterinary treatment, the fatality rate among afflicted felines is between 80 and 90 percent.

Equally frequent and contagious, rhinotracheitis does not have a single cause but a variety of causes. The disease predominantly affects kittens in their first year of life. Severe inflammation, accompanied by fever and a purulent discharge from the nose and eyes, characterizes the disease, which is usually restricted to the upper bronchial tubes. Provided no serious complications occur in addition, for instance pneumonia, the cat stands a good chance of recovering.

**You can make your cat a comfortable sick bed from a thick layer of newspaper covered with an old blanket or large towel. It should be placed in a warm room—ideally, in the cat's favorite resting place.**

## What can you do about fleas?

Fleas are both easy and difficult to combat. Easy, because nowadays there are very effective treatments against fleas that are easy to apply; difficult because they keep popping up from who knows where. Cats that are allowed outside can wear a flea collar that delivers an active substance that deters fleas over a period of time. Although it doesn't happen often, a flea collar can, unfortunately, cause accidents: The collar can get caught and strangle the cat while it is climbing or slipping through someplace. Personally, I prefer a campaign against these mighty hoppers using sprays, liquids, or mousses. Spray the cat's bed and favorite resting places at fourteen-day intervals with flea spray. Don't spray the cat itself, or it might confuse the hiss of the spray with savage feline hissing and take to its heels in fright. For a case-by-case de-fleaing campaign, flea mousses and liquids are in the animal's best interests. Rub the mousse or liquid thoroughly into the cat's fur, even against the grain, to ensure that the treatment reaches the cat's skin. Be sure to follow the directions on the packaging so that your cat does not lick the mousse or liquid and suffer side effects from ingesting the poison. The occasional flea the cat will skillfully comb out of its fur itself with its little "flea teeth."

pleasant experiences with humans may be ruined as a lap animal for the rest of its life and may disappear at top speed under the sofa whenever a strange person approaches. Cats also have a pointed way of making their owners aware that the latter's conduct is not acceptable to them. A particularly effective method they resort to is to do their "business" right next to, not in, the litter box. This is often a formal protest about the lack of cleanliness of the litter box. It might also be a protest about the existence of a new family member or a change in household routine. Some cats refuse food after they have been given away by their owners, whether to a vacation kennel or to entirely new owners. In extreme circumstances, such a hunger strike may be maintained until utter exhaustion sets in, and is always a sign that the cat is suffering deeply because it feels "forsaken by God and the world."

A hitherto good-natured lap cat may sometimes change into an aggressive, prickly character. When the occasional scratches that are inflicted during lively play become serious and deliberate bite and scratch

**Modern street traffic is a serious threat to our cats. Thousands of cats are hit every year because they simply can't properly assess the danger of the gigantic, roaring "car creatures" racing by.**

## Behavioral Disorders

Cats are kind, easy to care for, clean housemates that can adapt to a wide variety of family situations without any problem. Still, the cat's amazing adaptability has its limits. Life in an inappropriate setting, or in a setting that doesn't allow the expression of its basic nature, means the animal is under constant stress. As with humans, excessive stress leads to illness. Cats may respond to stress by developing physical symptoms or neurotic disorders. A kitten that has un-

**A cat that, for lack of any other opportunity, climbs on wooden and upholstered furniture, or sharpens its claws on such furniture, is behaving perfectly normally and according to its own nature. While people concerned about sparing their furniture see offensive bad habits on the part of the animal in such behavior, there is really no question of a behavioral disorder.**

marks, it is often an expression of built-up aggression. This sometimes occurs when a cat that is active by nature doesn't have any opportunity to vent its hunting and fighting instincts. Sometimes appropriate toys can offer a remedy. If the change in temperament persists, it may be an indication of some other illness or disease, and the concerned cat owner should consult a veterinarian.

Cats do not indulge in abnormal behavior merely because they want to annoy their human families. Far from it. Behavioral disorders are really nothing more than cries for help. The cat is making it clear that the responses to its emotional demands are anything but suitable for its feline nature. The people the cat is appealing to should respond by examining and changing their own ways of doing things so that their cat's species specific needs can be fulfilled as far as possible.

## The Life Expectancy of a Cat

Although the vernacular stubbornly insists that cats have nine lives, up until now scientists haven't been able to find out anything about lives number two through nine. It may, therefore, be supposed that the cat's first life is also its only life. The length of a cat's life depends to a large extent on the way of life and breed of cat. It also depends, of course, on the cat's personal predisposition, that is to say, on the cat's penchant for illness or accident. In general, indoor cats are allotted longer lives than their free-ranging counterparts. Extensive studies on the life span of cats have produced the following results. Cats kept exclusively indoors on the average reach an age of between twelve and fifteen years; cats with access to the outdoors, eight to ten years; and completely free-ranging cats, about six years. These figures are the mean, it should be noted. Especially outside, many cats prematurely fall victim to accident or disease. On the other hand, among sheltered family cats optimally tended by a veterinarian, Methuselahs over twenty years old are no longer

## An ounce of prevention is worth more than a pound of cure

Modern veterinary medicine has extremely effective yet easily tolerated vaccines at its disposal with which your cat can be protected from the worst viral diseases. For your cat's sake, you should at least follow through conscientiously with the vaccination program recommended by your veterinarian against feline distemper, rhinotracheitis (usually included in the distemper shot), and rabies. The vaccination against rabies is also in your own best interest, as an infection by this disease can be fatal for people as well. It should also be noted, though, that even for vaccinated cats that go outdoors there is still a certain—extremely slight—risk remaining of infection by rabies. If the cat is involved in a fight with and bitten by a rabid animal, say a fox, the cat itself might not suffer from rabies, but it could transmit the disease for some time through biting.

a rarity. The record age for a house cat, for which we have documentation, lies around thirty-six years. This instance involved a certain feline lady named Puss, who is recorded to have lived from 1903 to 1939. Still, her case is undoubtedly an extreme exception.

Among purebred cats, Siamese and Burmese cats are definitely long-lived. Many others, especially overbred purebreds, clearly have shorter life expectancies than mixed-breeds. The reason for this lies in the high rate of inbreeding of these "blue bloods."

Neutering extends the life expectancy of tomcats. Regardless of whether cats have access to the outdoors or not, castrated toms have a high probability of outliving their intact counterparts by quite a few years.

**There can be various reasons for a cat to suddenly stop being clean about its eliminations (ABOVE). An organic illness can be at the root of this just as easily as a heavy psychological burden. In this latter case, the cat expresses its loss of emotional balance through abnormal behavior. The aberrance, which is usually limited to depositing urine not feces, should therefore be understood as a cry for help and under no circumstances be seen as bad behavior.**

**Spray markings by tomcats (BELOW), and also some female cats, inside the house correspond to primal instinctive behavior. To the people, with whom the cat shares its territory, it may well stink, but it is, however, neither sickliness nor a behavioral disorder. The only remedy is neutering the animal—and even that is not always effective.**

**Whereas we people spend roughly a third of our lifetime in childhood and youth, a third as adults, and a third in old age, a cat will be grown up after about a tenth of its (average) life span, and is noticeably old only during the final tenth of its lifetime. A young Siamese kitten (ABOVE); a mature Siamese female (RIGHT).**

## Cats – a danger to pregnant women?

Should a pregnant woman be living in the company of a cat, the question about toxoplasmosis quickly comes to mind. This extremely common infection is caused by a single-celled parasite, a protozoan by the name of *Toxoplasma gondii,* and is usually like a mild flu. It can infect birds and mammals, including people. At a certain stage, the parasite metamorphoses into a very resistant, long-lasting form (so-called cysts) that are deposited and mature in the muscles or are eliminated with the feces. Infection usually takes place with the ingestion of contaminated meat, but also—and herein lies the danger to cat owners—in the eliminated cysts, which dry up into dust and then spread around everywhere in the vicinity of a cat. Anyone who has experienced the infection once (most often without even noticing it at all) is immune to recurrence. This applies, in our part of the world, to about two-thirds of all people. Should the initial infection occur during pregnancy, in half the cases the unborn baby will be infected as well. Without treatment there can be lasting damage to the brain and retinas of the unborn child. An expectant mother should let her doctor administer a blood test for toxoplasmosis antibodies at the beginning of her pregnancy. This will establish whether she is already immune or not. In the case that she is, there is no cause for worry. Should no immunity be evident, cautious observance of hygienic measures in dealing with cats, especially their litter boxes, is advised. All things considered, if the expectant mother has timely medical check-ups, the combination of pregnancy and a cat is no cause for family panic and honestly no cause to get rid of the cat. (Incidentally, infection by the toxoplasmosis parasite is much more probable through the consumption of raw or undercooked pork than by means of a cat.)

## A Cat's Twilight Years

Typically, the first signs of aging are noticeable in most cats when they jump and when they wash themselves. The joints stiffen up gradually and the movements of the hitherto wonderfully supple body slow down. Jumping, in particular, takes increased effort. The once-powerful legs have weakened, so that when the cat tries to jump up it tumbles down again with a ponderous thump. It can get to the point where a feline Methuselah has to be lifted up onto its favorite chair. It hardly need be said that so frail a cat can survive

only under human care. Whether it lives in the city or in the country, it no longer has any chance of catching enough prey to be self-sufficient, not the least because of the gaps already showing between its teeth. The stiffer the body becomes, the harder it gets for the cat to groom its fur, even in the few more accessible places. Soon the fur loses its sheen and quickly starts looking unkempt and neglected. As with aging people, the aging cat's sense of hearing and power of sight gradually diminish. The lenses of the cat's eyes lose their elasticity due to a build-up of connective tissue. This accumulation of connective tissue makes the eyes of very old cats appear blue-gray. In addition, the rods and cones in the retina of the cat's eye are less and less responsive, so that overall the cat loses its vision. The functioning of the internal organs decrease as well, starting with the kidneys and the liver. Underactivity of the intestines more often than not leads to serious blockages. Tumors can grow in just about any part of the body. In short: The cat's body visibly deteriorates.

The cat now sleeps even longer than before. It prefers a place nearer the radiator, as its need for warmth increases as well. The brain functions are also on the wane. The number of gray cells decreases so much

**With increasing age, many cats become honest-to-goodness grouches and hate to be disturbed during their increasingly lengthy periods of rest. Playful little kittens get a message that is abundantly clear.**

that the brain at the end of a cat's life is 25 percent lighter than it was during its prime. The transmission of signals in the nervous system operates with increasing sluggishness. In fact, an aged cat often responds so haltingly, it's as if it were just "slow on the uptake." Senility doesn't make itself evident only through physical symptoms. The mental flexibility isn't what it used to be, either. An old cat can come to terms with changes in the environment only with great difficulty—whether they be an addition to the family, new living room decor, or even a move. It is concerned about hanging onto its daily routine so that it can proceed as uniformly as possible. Even cats that have had a gregarious disposition all their lives can, when they age, turn into grumpy old loners who will most likely be extremely crotchety with others of their kind.

Should the cat's life become intolerable despite all our care and attention, we should consider saying good-bye. The final trip to the veterinarian is surely a painful one, but in trying to offer your cat a fitting life, it is also fitting to spare it a lengthy period of ailing, and, when its time has come, to grant it a merciful death.

**Old age doesn't pass cats by without a trace, either. Some get fat, but most lose weight in their later years. Typical, especially of females, is a sagging paunch, which makes the gauntness of the flanks even more evident. This venerable Siamese female is thirteen years old.**

# INDEX

# ABOUT THE AUTHORS

**Helga Hofmann** is a Ph.D. biologist who has worked for many years as a journalist and author of books on nature. In addition to her inquiries into general ecological subjects, Hofmann is interested in the subject of animal behavior research and keeps herself intensely busy with the biology and behavior of her house pets. For many years, she and her family have lived alongside house cats, and Hofmann says that her cats have brought her closer to catlike stamina and obstinateness regarding her own peculiarities and needs. Hofmann's personal experience with cats has enabled the text in *The Natural Cat: Understanding Your Cat's Needs and Instincts* to be easy to understand and entertaining while being based on the latest scientific knowledge.

**Monika Wegler** became a freelance photographer in 1983 and has published, as photographer and writer, more than seventeen books on the subject of animals. She has also worked as an illustrator in advertising and, for the last several years, on several dog and cat calendars. Her main areas of interest include house animals such as bunnies, dogs, and—naturally—cats. She lives with "four velvet paws" herself, who contributed to her work in this book. Wegler has included difficult-to-photograph subjects in *The Natural Cat: Understanding Your Cat's Needs and Instincts,* such as birth, hunting prey, pairing, and confrontations between strays.